THREE MODES
of
MODERN
SOUTHERN
FICTION

Ellen Glasgow

William Faulkner

Thomas Wolfe

THREE MODES
of MODERN
SOUTHERN
FICTION

Ellen Glasgow, William Faulkner,
Thomas Wolfe

C. HUGH HOLMAN

MERCER UNIVERSITY LAMAR
MEMORIAL LECTURES, NO. 9

UNIVERSITY OF GEORGIA PRESS
ATHENS

PS
379
,H64

To

MARGARET and DAVID
Daughter and Son of "Old Catawba,"
May It Be Yours to Know
"The Promise of America"

Contents

Foreword

IN THOMAS MORTON'S LATE-EIGHTEENTH-CENTURY COMEDY, *Speed the Plough,* whenever the slightest hint of impropriety is evident one of the characters invariably asks, "What will Mrs. Grundy say?" The Mercer University Lamar Lecture Committee often finds itself asking a similar question: "What would Mrs. Lamar say?" Many members of the present committee knew the donor of this lecture series personally, and the terms of her legacy "to provide the very highest type of scholarship which will aid in the permanent preservation of the values of Southern culture, history, and literature" are especially meaningful.

One can only conclude that Mrs. Lamar would have been particularly pleased with the series of lectures delivered by Professor C. Hugh Holman. A graceful writer, a stimulating speaker, and a thorough scholar-critic, Professor Holman goes about his task of delineating three distinct Souths with no hint of the iconoclast, but with a positive approach that sees his subject steadily and sees it whole. Professor Holman has provided a useful tool to any student of the South; instead of dealing with the multiplex voices of the area's cultures with one abstract term, the

"South," one may more realistically speak in terms of the Tidewater and Low Country South, the Piedmont and Mountain South, and the Gulf Coast or Deep South. His use of Ellen Glasgow, Thomas Wolfe, and William Faulkner as spokesmen for these three distinct cultural milieus made the lectures doubly rewarding. The unusually large and enthusiastic audiences of students and faculty members further attested to the effectiveness of this lecture series.

BENJAMIN W. GRIFFITH, JR., *Co-Chairman*
The Lamar Lecture Committee

Mercer University
Macon, Georgia

Preface

THE ESSAYS WHICH MAKE UP THIS VOLUME WERE DELIVERED
to groups of students, faculty members, and the general
public at Mercer University in Macon, Georgia, on No-
vember 15 and 16, 1965, as the Ninth Annual Series of
Eugenia Dorothy Blount Lamar Memorial Lectures. I
found the audience which I addressed to be alert and challenging and their comments and criticisms of the lectures
extremely useful to me.

As I now present these lectures in a slightly longer form
to an audience of readers, I feel that it is perhaps appropriate to acknowledge the limits which I imposed upon
myself in preparing these lectures and the assumptions
upon which they rest.

I believe that I have been more deeply influenced by
H. A. Taine's basic assumptions in *The History of English
Literature*[1] than those of any other critic whom I have
read. Taine's methods of presentation and interpretation
—although certainly capable of being grossly misused, even
by their creator—remain for me a fruitful way to examine
the nature and significance of literary works. As Edmund
Wilson says in his enthusiasm for *The History of English*

Literature, Taine "created the creators themselves as characters in a larger drama of cultural and social history."[2]

I should like here to give the controlling ideas of Taine's theory in his own words. He says, "Three different sources contribute to produce [an] elementary moral state—RACE, SURROUNDING, and EPOCH. What we call the race are the innate and hereditary dispositions which man brings with him into the world, and which, as a rule, are united with the marked differences in the temperament and structure of the body." By "surroundings," Taine means the social and physical structure within which the writer lives and works. He says, "For man is not alone in the world . . . accidental and secondary tendencies overlay his primitive tendencies, and physical or social circumstances disturb or confirm the character committed to their charge." The third of Taine's causes he calls the "epoch," a name that he uses for "the acquired momentum of a culture." He says, "When the national character and surrounding circumstances operate, it is not upon a *tabula rasa,* but on a ground on which marks are already impressed. According as one takes the ground at one moment or another, the imprint is different."[3]

In the essays which follow, I have tried to suggest in the broadest sense the way in which race, geography, climate, and religion have formed three relatively definite societies in the South. I have also attempted to suggest that continuing literary traditions and social attitudes have shaped, qualified, and, to some extent, defined the artistic methods and forms which writers in these regions have used. In order to demonstrate these things, I have attempted a generalized definition of regions and have sought in three novelists to trace what I believe to be the effect of "surrounding" in M. Taine's sense of that word.

In suggesting, as I do here, that there are three distinct regions that have produced definite variations in Southern society, I realize that I am oversimplifying a very complex geographical, historical, and social pattern and that the areas which I define overlap each other to a very notable extent. At the same time that this process of oversimplification is going on, I believe that it serves as a partial corrective for a larger oversimplification which has commonly been made. There is an area which can accurately be called "The South" though its outer land boundaries are indefinite and hazy. Within that larger area, as a result of mountains, climate, and race, there are three societies only shadowily defined at their outer limits but distinct and sharp at their centers. These Souths may be called the Tidewater and Low Country South, the Piedmont and Mountain South, and the Gulf Coast or Deep South. Each of these sub-regions has found, I believe, distinctive representation in the work of the best writers which each has produced in this century. I have accordingly chosen Ellen Glasgow as the spokesman for the Tidewater South and as a writer whose work reflects the impact of that region upon her art; I have chosen Thomas Wolfe as a writer who reflects the Piedmont and Mountain South and whose work shows the impact of that region upon his art; and I have chosen William Faulkner as a writer dealing with the Deep South whose work is shaped at its very center by the characteristics of his region.

I have elected to assist the student and, hopefully, reassure the skeptical reader in their efforts to verify my sources by footnoting specific references in the text and by including at the end a "Note on Sources." My reason for this method is that many of the things I have to say about the South, its history, and its structure are drawn from several different works and are put together here as a result of my own attempts to merge and order the views of several historians and literary critics. Thus, at any given point a specific footnote hardly indicates truly the variety of sources with which I am dealing. I hope that my "Note on Sources" will lead the reader to pursue for himself the growing body of sophisticated comment on the nature, quality, and meaning of the South, both as a literary subject and as a personal and often tragic experience.

I wish, too, to express my gratitude to Mercer University, the Trustees of the Eugenia Dorothy Blount Lamar Memorial Lectures, and the faculty of Mercer for the honor which they did me in inviting me to deliver these lectures. I am particularly indebted to Professor Ben W. Griffith, Jr., who, as co-chairman of the committee on the lectures, was a gracious and stimulating host. Many hands too numerous to mention went into the slow formulation of the basic ideas which I am attempting to suggest in these essays; but I would like, in particular, to express my appreciation to the graduate students in my courses at Chapel Hill, and especially in my course in Southern American Literature, for the assistance they have given me in ordering my thoughts and the high compliment which they have paid me by actively challenging my notions and forcing me to think them through. I owe a special and very great debt to my secretary, Mrs. Letitia Curtis, who not only typed my manuscript, corrected my syntax, and verified my quotations, but brought to the essays themselves a friendly but critical eye; they are far better because of her efforts.

C. HUGH HOLMAN

Chapel Hill, North Carolina
December 1, 1965

ONE

Diversity Within Unity

> . . . it was my original intention to depict such
> aspects of the Southern scene as I had actually known,
> and to avoid the romantic delusion . . . that the South
> was inhabited exclusively by aristocrats and pic-
> tureque Negroes . . .   *Ellen Glasgow*[4]

IT IS A TRUISM THAT ALL GENERALIZATIONS TEND TO STRIP
from concrete actualities their distinctive individual characteristics, for generalizations define a class in terms not
of the unique values of its separate members but of common qualities which they share. The word "cow," to use
Count Alfred Korzybski's figure,[5] does not describe a
unique thing that might be called "Bossie" but an infinite
number of "Bossies" of various shapes, colors, and tempers;
yet the term "cow" is certainly more precise than
"quadruped," which not only strips Bossie of her identity
but strips her entire family of identity, grouping her with
all four-legged animals.

The term "The South" is in certain respects similar.
There is no real "South" except as a high level abstraction
within which land, language, race, climate, mountain and

1

plain, pine and palm are mixed together in a common conception. Yet this abstraction "The South" obviously has social, historical, political, and literary value, for the southeastern United States has maintained an homogeneity of belief and commitment and has held a dream of a traditional social order with sufficient consistency to set it aside as a distinctive portion of a nation, which, in large measure, has itself been free from the obsessions with order and with the past which would have distinguished the South, even had it never tried by force of arms to assert its separateness.

The only other region of the United States that has maintained as intense a self-conscious distinctiveness has been New England in the first two-thirds of the nineteenth century, when Puritan theology, ethical fervor, and an intense commitment to the strenuous moral life gave it a unique identity, a separate integrity, and a common view. The South during this same period was also assuming a distinctive regional nature and attempting to create and to preserve its own concept of the good life. Among the causes for this separateness was a climate that made the region a healthy site for an agrarian economy, the presence of slavery as a working basis for the Cotton Kingdom, the embracing of politics and law as the highest reaches of a culture, and an emphasis on good manners and gracious living. Where New England aspired to moral earnestness, as it embraced industrialism and embarked on the path to urbanization, the South elected the Agrarian way and modeled itself on the English squire-archy. While John Bunyan would have felt himself at home in Massachusetts, Sir Roger de Coverley would have understood the system which the South aspired to build.

The sense of regional identity which set the mind of the rural South against the larger nation almost from the beginning was rooted in the past, in the sequence of historical events which resulted in the desperate effort between 1861 and 1865 to utter an enduring "No" to the national dream. All parts of the South in their differing ways embraced this passion for separate identity and shared the common dream of "a Caribbean empire," which found its first powerful expression in the Mexican War and Taylor's race for the presidency, so that 1848 became a water shed in Southern history and 1865 became the catastrophic end to the dream of a separate culture and a separate nation.

It is relatively easy after winning a war to forgive your late enemies and to forget the conflict, as America's allies in two world wars have learned and as Japanese gardens, furniture, art, and motorcycles make sometimes painfully obvious to the contemporary citizen. On the other hand, a lost war remains a permanent affront to the honor and the dignity of the people who lost it. In the broad sweep of human history, few triumphant causes have permanently lived for long in the minds of the victors; but there are long records of the embittered survival of lost causes. As C. Vann Woodward has cogently argued many times, the most distinctive single characteristic of the southeastern United States is that it has undergone an experience not shared by the rest of the nation—that of having fought and lost a war, having endured reconstruction, and having lived with poverty, defeat, and frustration as a part of the bread it ate and the blood it shared.[6] The past has been something that the South has not been able to forget, whether that past is seen as symbolized by the timeless and almost imperceptible decay of three-story-high and one-room-deep houses facing toward Charleston's rivers, whether it is seen as symbolized by a series of events named Shiloh, Vicksburg, Gettysburg, Atlanta, or whether it is seen in terms of the grim strategies of "grandfather clauses" and the cruel invention of "Jim Crow." This sense of the past, this sense that what has gone before has stripped from the inhabitants of the region a substantial portion of their own freedom to act, has given the South in our time a view of the meaning of life that is darkened by a sense of shame and deepened by the tragic awareness of human failure and of pain. Thus the South has been and is different from the rest of the nation.

Yet, although the Southern region, in this sense, has had a unique identity, the term "South" is too broad an abstraction to be handled with very much precision by its historians or its critics. There are not one but many Souths; and these many fall, at the next level of abstraction into a three-part grouping made by geographical differences, major variations in social patterns, and various strains of race and culture resulting from different kinds and times of migration, so that "The South" is comprised of at least three distinct sub-regions with radical differences among themselves—differences almost as great as those between the total region and the rest of the nation. These sub-regions certainly overlap at many points, and they share many common characteristics, so that, except for the extreme forms of each of these sub-regions, they seem to shade into each other almost imperceptibly, despite the fact that each maintains a geographical distinctiveness.

Geographically the southeastern United States consists of a broad coastal plain rich in rivers and readily accessible to those who boarded frighteningly frail crafts and sailed them over unknown seas to Roanoke Island, into the James River, and into the Cooper and Ashley Rivers at Charleston. At the edge of the Atlantic coastal plain is the "fall line," a geological formation which separates the plain from the rolling hills. This fall line passes through Richmond, Virginia; Raleigh, North Carolina; Columbia, South Carolina; and Milledgeville, Georgia. Behind it the gentle rise of the Piedmont stretches westward until it suddenly flings itself skyward to form the Southern Appalachian and Blue Ridge Mountains. Westward from the first ranges of the Blue Ridge and the Appalachian Mountains is the Great Valley. The entire southeastern region is bounded on the east and south by the Atlantic and Gulf coastal plains and is marked latitudinally by climate variations. Virginia, the Carolinas, Tennessee, and much of Georgia are in a humid, warm, temperate zone. Florida, Alabama, Mississippi, and Louisiana are in a humid semi-tropical zone. Hence we can, with some accuracy, talk of a temperate coastal South—variously called the Tidewater and the Low Country—of a Piedmont South which extends into and includes the Appalachian and Blue Ridge Mountains, and of a Deep South which is largely a semi-tropical Gulf Coast plain.

These geographical distinctions were reflected, too, in the immigrants who first inhabited these sections and by the nature of the receding frontier in the South. The Atlantic coastal plain was generally settled by British colonists of Cavalier leanings. The malcontents, the failures, and the criminals from the coastal establishment moved into the hill country and the mountain sections where they joined the sturdy and independent Scotch-Irish, who entered through Northern ports and came down the Great Valley from Pennsylvania along with the Germans and the Irish, to shape the general social structure of the Piedmont region. The Gulf Coast plain was settled much later. At first it was reserved for the Indians; then it became the home of those moving westward and southward from both established cultures, that of the coastal British and that of the Piedmont Scotch-Irish. There in the sub-tropics the combination of rich soil and an imperfectly transmitted dream of plantation glory gave to the Deep South a somewhat distorted version of the characteristics of the Tidewater world.

W. J. Cash has described these three Souths as they stood at the end of the Revolution with graceful concision: first there was the Atlantic Coastal plain South—"a narrow world, confined to the areas where tobacco, rice, and indigo could profitably be grown on a large scale." Next comes the vast backcountry of the seaboard settlements: "there lived unchanged the pioneer breed—the unsuccessful and the restless from the older regions; the homespun Scotch-Irish . . . the pious Moravian brothers . . . stolid Lutheran peasants from northern Germany; ragged, throat-slitting Highlanders . . . [a] generally unpretentious and often hard-bitten crew . . . [whose lives were] still largely a matter of coon-hunting, of 'painter' tales and hard drinking." Mr. Cash, moving toward a third Southern region, says, ". . . all the country which was to be Alabama, Mississippi, western Georgia, and northern Louisiana, was still mainly a wasteland, given over to the noble savage and peripatetic traders with an itch for adventure and a taste for squaw seraglios."[7]

That these three regions shaped markedly the response of their inhabitants to the common pressures of history which they shared—indeed, so shaped them that frequently equivalent forces produced opposing results—accounts for a multiplicity rather than a unity in the Southern world; for each of these regions and groups created a distinctive society. However shadowy the lines of demarcation among them may be and however similar many of their attitudes were, they dreamed different dreams, formulated different social structures, and worshipped different gods. These differences have persisted for a century and a half and they give evidence of being qualities permanent to their various locales.

In addition to these three Souths, we could enumerate many others; but they would be subclasses under these three. Many Southern historians and critics of Southern literature, ignoring the extent and the intensity of these differences, have assumed the existence of a homogeneity in the southeastern United States which has never existed. These differences become obvious when the region's social assumptions are put under test. Since the Supreme Court decision on Civil Rights in 1954, each of these Souths has been subjected to a social and moral test of great intensity and consistency. Only one who has failed to note the differences in the reactions of these sub-regions can assume that the South has been uniform in its pattern of response; and those who think they can see a Wallace or a Barnett in Atlanta or in North Carolina simply have overlooked the historical, racial, and social differentia of these three sub-regions. On a simpler and more obvious level, one needs only to visit the ideal and orderly Tidewater as it has been reconstructed at Williamsburg, Virginia, and contrast that way of life to that reconstructed in Old Salem, in Winston-Salem, North Carolina, in order to see that these rebuilt Colonial villages are poles apart in almost every sense of the word.

When the South becomes, as it has in our time, the subject of important literary works, each of its sub-regions provides a different subject matter to the novelist. The combinations of subject matter, the authors' talents, and their personal relationships to their regions result in distinctive fictional modes. H. A. Taine's "race, surroundings, and epoch" differ markedly in each sub-region; and the result is a radical—through not always recognized—difference in the works of fiction shaped by the various sub-regions.

This distinctiveness is pervasive and almost total, for the Southern novelists of the twentieth century have not shared the historians' and the critics' limited views. Good novelists are not interested in abstractions. They are interested in the direct and powerful communication of

intense emotion through the representation of characters
and actions; and if there are three distinct modes of
Southern fiction corresponding to three sub-Souths, they
are to be found on the most effective level among the
representative writers who have tried to describe and have
themselves been shaped by the essential attributes of each
of these three sub-regions. I have elected to try to examine
these three modes in selected works by Ellen Glasgow,
Thomas Wolfe, and William Faulkner, each of whom is,
I believe, the finest novelist of his sub-region.

In other places I have argued that there exists a group
of literary characteristics, some sizeable accumulation of
which constitute a "Southern literary tradition"; and I
have been insistent, too, that Ellen Glasgow and Thomas
Wolfe belong to that tradition, as clearly William Faulkner does. Among these characteristics are a sense of evil,
a pessimism about man's potential, a tragic sense of life,
a deep-rooted sense of the interplay of past and present,
a peculiar sensitivity to time as a complex element in
narrative art, a sense of place as a dramatic dimension, and
a thoroughgoing belief in the intrinsic value of art as an
end in itself, with an attendant Aristotelian concern with
forms and techniques.[8] In varying degrees, each of these
three novelists represents a significantly large combination
of these traits; yet none of them would have been happy
to be thus lumped together, and all of them probably
would endorse Flannery O'Connor's irritated assertion
that "The woods are full of regional writers, and it is the
great horror of every serious Southern writer that he will
become one of them."[9]

The most articulate formulators of a notion of Southern
distinctiveness were the group at Vanderbilt University
who published *The Fugitive* magazine and somewhat
ostentatiously in 1930 "took their stand" against indus-

trialism and modern America. These writers—the most important of whom were John Crowe Ransom, Allen Tate, Donald Davidson, and Robert Penn Warren—looked with only very limited favor on Miss Glasgow and Thomas Wolfe; and, although they praised Faulkner (who ranked Wolfe as the best of his contemporaries) and have been, on the whole, his best critics (especially Robert Penn Warren and Cleanth Brooks),[10] Faulkner was not truly a part of their movement. Each of these writers could look with some sense of detachment and even with an element of mild distaste at the Fugitive-Agrarians, whom Wolfe once called "the refined young gentlemen of the New Confederacy . . . [who] retired haughtily into the South, to the academic security of a teaching appointment at one of the universities from which they could issue in quarterly installments very small and very precious magazines which celebrated the advantages of an agrarian society."[11]

The subject of these essays is really the impact of the cultures of these three sub-regions on three Southern novelists of great talent and substantial accomplishment and in turn the distinctively different views of the South which each of these novelists embodies in his own work. Ellen Glasgow wrote of the Tidewater South in novels of manners laid in Richmond, thinly disguised in her fiction as Queenborough. Thomas Wolfe, himself the product of the union of the Pennsylvania German and the Scottish Southern mountain settler, spoke powerfully and distinctly of the Piedmont South and its way of life. For the Deep South, William Faulkner defined through his vast record of Yoknapatawpha County the vain and often frenzied efforts of ambitious but "innocent" men to establish a tradition of honor and integrity upon the soil of Mississippi and the backs of Negro slaves. Out of their failure, he fashions not only a record of the Deep South but also a tragedy of human ambition, perhaps as deeply rooted in universal experience as any has ever been in our national literature.

My method will be to select from each author works that are generally considered to be among his best and which reflect the special qualities of his sub-region, those qualities which differentiate it from the other sub-regions. I shall then attempt to relate each of these works to the broad characteristics of the sub-region with which it deals, to the works of other writers who have dealt with similar subject matter, and to its author's career, hoping by this method that the novels will help to reveal the quality of their sub-regions and also that the sub-regions will assist us in seeing a little more clearly than before the aspects of the work which help to create one of its meanings— basically the meaning which grows from the interplay of art and social subject.

Such a method seems to me not only defensible but desirable, for the social qualities of the Southern novel are, although not ends in themselves, still important parts of what Henry James called the author's *donnèe*.

T W O

Ellen Glasgow: The Novelist of Manners as Social Critic

> . . . even her realm of phantasy was a small, enclosed province, peopled by skeletons of tradition and governed by a wooden theology.
>
> *Ellen Glasgow*[12]

THE OLDEST CULTURE PRODUCED BY ENGLISH-SPEAKING PEOPLE in the Colonial South was that of Tidewater Virginia, a region settled in large measure as an economic enterprise by English adventurers who were financed by large trading companies and who brought with them not only the inclination to name their new lands in honor of their old monarchs—the Virgin Queen and James and William—but also to create, so far as in them lay, a social order as nearly like that of the British aristocracy as they found to be possible. Perhaps few of these Tidewater explorers and colonizers carried within their veins the blood of noble families, but most of them carried within their brains the dream of noble orders; and the Cavalier tradition in government, the Episcopal tradition in religion, the pragmatic profit motive in philosophy, and the hedonistic aim in social customs helped to establish along the Atlantic

11

seaboard a South of hierarchal values and class and caste
distinctions.

In the latter part of the century, other Englishmen came
to settle the lands assigned by Charles II to the Lords
Proprietors, and they created at the confluence of the
Cooper and Ashley Rivers a city called Charleston and a
culture which finally resulted from the mingling of several
races—among them the English, the Spanish Jews, the
French Huguenots, and the Irish immigrants. This society
achieved a quality in Colonial times that made South
Carolinians aspire, as Henry Adams notes, "to a desire
to other distinctions than those which could be earned
at the bar or on the plantation." As Adams said in his
monumental *History of the United States During the
Administrations of Jefferson and Madison,* "The small society of rice and cotton planters at Charleston, with their
cultivated tastes and hospitable habits, delighted in whatever reminded them of European civilization. They were
travellers, readers, and scholars; the society of Charleston
compared well in refinement with that of any city of its
size in the world, and English visitors long thought it the
most agreeable in America."[13]

At the area around Williamsburg, Jamestown, and
Richmond, there early developed a society of the tobacco-
aristocrats whose plantations stretched along the James
and its tributaries and formed the basis for a demanding
but urbane agrarian culture. There, as it had been in
South Carolina, the culture was established as a result of
what Thomas J. Wertenbaker called the four great factors
acting on Colonial society—foreign inheritance, local conditions, continued contact with Europe, and the melting
pot. By the end of the eighteenth century, as Wertenbaker
also points out, "the Boston merchant, the Virginia
tobacco aristocrat, the rice millionaire of South Carolina,
. . . had the time and the inclination to turn from the

counting room or the management of slaves or the disposing of crops to the higher things of life."[14]

At its noblest and best, in the vast rice plantations along the Ashley River, in estates like William Byrd's Westover, and in the genteel life antiseptically recreated in Mr. Rockefeller's Williamsburg, this Tidewater and Low Country culture was the closest thing to a society of fixed classes with an ideal of impeccable manners and gracious living that the North American hemisphere has ever known. That it was realized only in part, that it crested in colonial days and began its slow decline in the early years of the nineteenth century, and that it had more power as a dream and a faith than it did as a fact does not alter greatly—and, in fact, may enhance—its pervasive and continuing influence on America and Americans.

The attempt to create an actual order of social conduct, of manners, and of gracious living was unique among American societies. This order rested upon a caste system in society, upon an established religion, and upon a concept of honor which expressed itself primarily through manners. In this seaboard society there was little room for the skeptic, the cynic, the malcontent, or the criminal. The western frontier—and the "lubberland" of North Carolina—both welcomed and enticed these classes, so that those who remained had a remarkably large body of commonly held assumptions and ideals. Behind this relatively stable society was a way of life not far removed from the ideals of neoclassic England in the days of the country squire. Few Virginia or Carolina planters were American equivalents of Sir Roger de Coverley, but many of them knew the essays by Addison and Steele which made de Coverley a permanent part of the American as well as the British mind. This seaboard culture was perhaps as fruitful an area for the novel of manners as America has ever produced.

The term "novel of manners" describes a work in which

the outer forms of a relatively closed society are stable, so that a character may be tested against them as against a fairly inflexible yardstick of conduct and belief. At few times in the history of the modern world have adequate conditions existed for such novels of manners in an absolute sense. Jane Austen, writing of the country gentry in English rural villages in the days of the Napoleonic Wars, produced the most nearly absolute comedies of manners which the English language has known. Within her rural villages change occurred very slowly, and the English squirearchy defined a view of life being modified at a snail's pace; yet Jane Austen wrote during two decades of British history which produced the most radical changes in the structure of England which occurred before the Second World War. She sat in country parsonages while Napoleon dominated Europe and penned novels concerned essentially with marriage as a social institution; and while two brothers were in Nelson's fleet at Trafalgar, she continued to portray not the world of war but the same closed British society. Two years after her death, the Peterloo Massacre occurred; and fifteen years later the first of the great Reform Bills was passed by Parliament, so that Miss Austen's novels of manners were essentially novels which tested men and women in a sharply arrested moment in human history. In a world of dynamic change —and particularly in a democratic society—the novelist of manners must always seek such arrested moments. The adequacy of the Tidewater culture for such novels of manners has perhaps been approached in America only by the society of Knickerbocker New York and certain portions of New England. Thus it early attracted the attention of writers of fiction who were interested in preserving a record of its structure.

In 1832 John Pendleton Kennedy in *Swallow Barn* attempted to define the nature and the ideals of the Tidewater plantation society. His work was, as even he insisted, not a novel but a collection of fictional sketches describing life at Swallow Barn, "an aristocratical old edifice which sits, like a brooding hen, on the southern bank of the James River."[15] Behind Kennedy's view of life on the plantation was the example of Washington Irving's attempt in *Bracebridge Hall* to define the conventions, customs, and eccentricities of the British squire. Kennedy's book has often been regarded as the first fictional document in the creation of the concept of a plantation tradition. It was followed by the work of many other writers, and Virginia became the subject for a representation of a society with a social structure resting upon a tradition of manners. This structure found its expression in many different ways over the years of change. Thomas Nelson Page, in *In Ole Virginia*, a collection of short stories, and in the novel *Red Rock*, gave this society an idealized and sentimental treatment through which he presented an apologia for the vanished South. He once said that this South "partook of the philosophical tone of the Grecian, of the dominant spirit of the Roman, and of the guardfulness of individual rights of the Saxon civilization. And over all brooded a softness and beauty, the joint product of Chivalry and Christianity."[16] It was thus, as Ellen Glasgow saw, that "the spirit of adventure had disintegrated into an evasive idealism, a philosophy of heroic defeat."[17]

James Branch Cabell attempted in a long series of novels under the collective title *The Biography of the Life of Manuel* to pick up the themes of such a society, to trace them through an imaginary European country, and finally to bring them to Virginia and in particular to Lichfield, a city very much like Richmond. The themes he chose were the chivalrous, the gallant, and the poetic; and in applying them to his imaginary world, he saw the chivalrous as a testing, the gallant as a toy, and the poetic as raw material. The finest of these novels dealing with Virginia were *The Cream of the Jest: A Comedy of Evasions, The Rivet in Grandfather's Neck: A Comedy of Limitations,* and *The Cords of Vanity: A Comedy of Shirking.* Cabell was consciously constructing through an art a world that was remote, ironically romantic, and, finally, strongly suggestive of an ideal. He believed that only in the effort to assert the impossible through a dream can we begin to approach making that dream in any sense real. Thus one of his novelist-characters declares that he is writing "an apology for romance by a man who believes that romance is dead beyond resurrection"; and particularly in his Virginia novels Cabell presents in each book a protagonist who "after his alloted jaunt, with youth to incite him, into outlandish regions, accepts more or less willingly his allotted place in the social organisms of his own people and country."[18]

It was to this South that Ellen Glasgow looked in her long career as a novelist; and out of its structure of manners undergoing steady attrition through the rise of the middle class, she made both serious fiction and comic novels. In the world about her she thought she saw that "What distinguished the Southerner, and particularly the Virginian, from his severer neighbours to the north was his ineradicable belief that pleasure is worth more than toil, that it is worth more even than profit. Although the difference between the Virginian and the far Southerner was greater than the distance between Virginia and Massachusetts, a congenial hedonism had established in the gregarious South a confederacy of the spirit."[19] Thus the Tidewater South became for her "a living tradition decayed, with the passage of years, into a sentimental infirmity." She knew that by and large this old South did not exist, that it had "vanished from the world of fact to reappear in the permanent realm of fable. . . . What we are in danger of forgetting," she said, "is that few possessions are more precious than a fable that no longer can be compared with a fact."[20] It is out of that fable that she fashioned her best work; and the result is that the most obvious serious artistic use which has so far been made of Virginia as a subject for the novel of manners has been the work of Ellen Glasgow.

In the long series of novels which she published between 1897 and 1941, she attempted to produce a body of work which spanned the social history of Virginia from the Civil War to the present. She said, "I began a history of manners that would embrace those aspects of Southern life with which I was acquainted . . . I planned to portray the different social orders, and especially, for this would constitute the major theme of my chronicle, the rise of the middle class as the dominant force in Southern democracy."[21] Whether this intention of Miss Glasgow's indeed existed clearly in her mind as early as 1897 and continued on until the 1940's is a matter of substantial debate. Her friend, James Branch Cabell, has declared that he suggested to Miss Glasgow that she arrange her work in this historical pattern in the late 1920's and that she embraced the idea and made it retroactive. She has, of course, had gallant defenders against Mr. Cabell's unchivalrous remarks, and the truth seems to lie somewhere between.[22] Probably she did with only partial consciousness, attempt to construct a fictional history of her state and then after the fact embraced the firm idea when Mr. Cabell pointed out to her the presence of many characteristics of social history in her fiction. She arranged into three groups the thirteen novels she valued most highly of the nineteen books of fiction which she produced. The first of these groups consisted of six novels of the Commonwealth, in which she sketches the history of Virginia from 1850 to

1912. The second group consists of three novels of the country, which span the period between 1898 and 1933 and which deal with the changing agrarian culture of rural Virginia with a substantial emphasis upon those people of good character, strong effort, and pietistic religion whom she called "plain people" and to whom she attributed the qualities of respectability and sound common sense. (She seems to have shared the belief of General Archbald in *The Sheltered Life* that they are people "who could be trusted in revolutions."²³) The third group is made up of four novels of the city—three of them tragi-comedies of manners; the fourth was a final and despairing farewell to an urban life in which beauty, dignity, and value can be found only in the enduring sacrifice of oppressed people.

She felt that she had written her best books after 1922. These books were *Barren Ground* (1925), a Hardyesque narrative of Dorinda Oakley who personified in the country "the spirit that fought with gallantry and gaiety, and that in defeat remained undefeated";²⁴ *The Romantic Comedians* (1926), a comedy of manners laid in Queenborough; *They Stooped to Folly* (1929), a Queenborough comedy of marriage; *The Sheltered Life* (1932), a tragi-comedy laid in Queenborough; *Vein of Iron* (1935), a grim novel of the country; and *In This Our Life* (1941), a dark novel of the city. She regarded *The Sheltered Life* and *Barren Ground* as her two finest novels, and her judgment has been accepted by most of her critics.²⁵

Ellen Glasgow was both the self-conscious spokesman for the Seaboard Southern culture and at the same time one of its sharpest critics. For her the tradition of manners and the pattern of conduct which the Tidewater South had produced served the function of making those tests of character and of custom upon which she wished to expend her energies. She was a part of the region of which she wrote and lived most of her life in Richmond.

She was caught up herself in a pattern of behavior common to the patrician citizen of the post-Civil War world; and yet it was a world whose traditions seemed to her to have survived as empty forms long after the demise of the moral convictions and the ethical systems which originally had called them forth.

Her subject matter, as she herself defined it, was the "retreat of an agararian culture before the conquests of an industrial revolution, and the slow and steady rise of the lower middle class."[26] From the beginning of her career, irony was the device which she used to lay bare the inner nature of the social order which was her subject. The South's greatest needs, she declared, were "blood and irony." "Blood," she said, "because Southern culture had strained too far away from its roots in the earth"; and irony because she thought it to be "the safest antidote to sentimental decay."[27] That her society was one in which tradition had solidified into meaningless postures made it, she felt, a proper subject for comedies and tragi-comedies of manners, for she saw everywhere about her what she called "a tone of manners [which] rang hollow [because] the foundations of the old aristocratic order . . . had never safely settled back on their corner-stone of tradition."[28]

It is in the three comedies of manners, *The Romantic Comedians, They Stooped to Folly,* and *The Sheltered Life,* that she dealt most effectively with the manners and traditions of the Tidewater after they had reached a state of decay; and the representation of the impact of this stultifying tradition thus becomes the major subject of her novels of the city. This tradition creates a way of life at a price that is extremely high. At one point in *The Sheltered Life,* she writes about "the code of perfect behaviour [which] supported her as firmly as if it had been a cross."[29] Most of her characters are, like Judge Gamaliel Honeywell in *The Romantic Comedians,* representations of Virginia society, "spritely in speech . . . ceremonious in manner."[30] The judge had, she felt, been "Southern in sentiment, yet not provincial in thought, he had attached himself to the oppressed minority . . . the urbane and unprejudiced South."[31] However, he was, she felt, "disposed to encourage liberty of thought as long as he was convinced that it did not lead to liberal views."[32] This kind of society ultimately shaped a conventional mind that was safe from the onslaught of reality. The people who made up her social world, Miss Glasgow felt, were like Mrs. Upchurch in *The Romantic Comedians,* who "had a small mind but knew it thoroughly," and they could "recite the Apostles' Creed so long as [they were] not required to practice the Sermon on the Mount, and could countenance Evolution until it threatened the image of its Maker."[33] She was, she declared, describing in these novels of manners "an epoch when faith and facts did not cultivate an acquaintance."[34]

She was a polished craftsman, and her effort to describe this society was one in which she exercised a very well developed and most effective literary artistry, and she was self-conscious about the extent to which the work she was doing differed from much fiction that was being written in her own time. She included many of her Southern contemporaries in the class of those who wrote without learning their craft first, as a painter might do when he never learned how to make his brush strokes. Faulkner's creations, for example, she regarded as "monstrous." In a querulous tone, she said, "Pompous illiteracy, escaped from some Freudian cage, is in the saddle, and the voice of the amateur is the voice of authority . . . To the poet, it is true, especially if he can arrange with destiny to die young, the glow of adolescence may impart an unfading magic. But the novel . . . requires more substantial ingredients than a little ignorance of life and a great yearning to tell everything one has never known."[35]

In keeping with this view, her novels of manners are well made and self-consciously written books. Behind almost every sentence can be heard the urbane voice of the novelist guiding the reader to consciousness of the final absurdity of lives surrendered to dead traditions. She said of *The Romantic Comedians* in one of her franker and less modest moments that she felt that as a comedy of manners it had never been surpassed in the novel form. Acknowledging that it was, she felt, "a slight novel," still she could maintain that within its limits it was nearly perfect.[36]

In her novels of manners, Ellen Glasgow repeatedly shows us men and women of wisdom and perception who lack the moral courage to act upon their knowledge and hence are destroyed by societies whose fundamental weakness they recognize but to which they bring not anger or resistance but amusement and retreat. Nowhere is this characteristic more obvious than in her novel *The Sheltered Life* where her protagonist, she claims, is General Archbald. She regards the General as an example of "the civilized mind in a world where even the civilizations we make are uncivilized";[37] and yet despite that kind of praise, General Archbald is finally a representative figure of his own world, a world that subscribes to a false idealism. At every crucial point he has lacked the quality of character which would have enabled him to make his civilized mind felt as an active force in his decaying civilization.

In *The Sheltered Life,* Miss Glasgow was attempting to examine Queenborough society through two opposing points of view. One is that of youth, personified in Jenny Blair Archbald, whose innocence and adolescent ignorance ultimately become the instruments of destruction. The other is age represented by General Archbald, who views at the end of a long life the conflict of tradition with change and sees that the shelter which his fixed society has erected to protect its members against reality ultimately has failed despite the fact that from him it has elicited a cost that is far greater than any values it could have given in return. In his eighties he knows that "what he had wanted, he had never had; what he had wished to do, he had never done."[38] He had given up the woman whom he had loved because an accidental delay in a snowstorm had forced him to compromise another woman in the public view, although not in the private fact. She was a woman for whom he had much respect but no affection, yet he followed the demands of tradition and married the "compromised" woman. Looking back across his past, he could declare, "Few men at eighty-three were able to look back upon so firm and rich a past, upon so smooth and variegated a surface. A surface! Yes, that, he realized now, was the flaw in the structure. Except for that one defeated passion in his youth, he had lived entirely upon the shifting surface of facts. He had been a good citizen, a successful lawyer, a faithful husband, an indulgent father; he had been, indeed, everything but himself. Always he had fallen into the right pattern; but the centre of the pattern was missing."[39] Jenny Blair says of him, "Grandfather has very queer notions. Mamma told me he was so queer when he was young that everybody was surprised when he made a good living. I asked him about that, and he laughed and said that he made a good living by putting an end to himself."[40]

General Archbald and Jenny Blair, youth and age, viewing a system that is rapidly passing away, are the instruments by which Miss Glasgow defines a view which she expressed in a letter about *The Sheltered Life*: "The two overlapping themes are . . . [that] we cannot put up a shelter against life and we kill what we love too much." By the term "sheltered life," Miss Glasgow meant, she said, "the whole civilization man has built to protect himself from reality";[41] and the harshest of the criticisms that she can level is implied in that statement, for it is the willing separation of her characters from reality which allows them finally to become the sources not of tragic power but of comic laughter.

In *They Stooped to Folly*, Miss Glasgow was, by her own definition, attempting to embody "one of the immemorial women-myths in a modern comedy of manners."[42] In this case, the myth was that of the "ruined woman" and the varying ways in which the tradition within which she lived expressed itself through its handling of her. *They Stooped to Folly* also demonstrates another of Miss Glasgow's methods of dissecting this society. In this novel she shows Mr. Littlepage and those who are around him as subservient to an imagined but sterile moral order. The title applies to three different instances in three succeeding generations of Oliver Goldsmith's lovely woman "who stoops to folly and finds too late that men betray." In three generations this "ruined woman" moves from the attic where the family imprions her in their joint disgrace to the center of the social scene where her moral error is almost a social asset. That Mr. Littlepage has given his life in support of an ideal of no more finality and longevity than this would be tragic if Mr. Littlepage had the appropriate "magnitude," to meet Aristotle's definition. The fate of a great man can be tragic; the same fate earned by a pleasant fool can be amusing; and Miss Glasgow is a skilled and sometimes malicious painter of male fools.

Each of these novels is close to the novel of manners even though none of them succeeds in completely realizing the full novel of manners as a form. The English novel

of manners is, as we have said, essentially a novel which
tests men and women by accepted standards of conduct in
a sharply arrested moment in history. Miss Glasgow had no
such arrested moment with which to deal. For her, life
itself and the lives of her characters were lived out at a
time when order and tradition, if they survived at all, had
to survive not as a meaningful or as a static ideal but
through a vain defiance of the great realities of social
change which made her world. Her comedies of manners,
therefore, if we can apply the term to them, are significantly different from those of Jane Austen, for Miss
Austen's world was a world of social conventions that
adequately reflected its inner beliefs about the nature and
interrelationship of men. Miss Glasgow's world was a
world in which the conventions had outlived the beliefs
which they once expressed. Hence, she could and did use
terms like "evasive idealism" and "sentimental decay" and
use them with accuracy. Her characters are tested not by
their conformity to a meaningful code but by their futile
rebellion against a dead one. Yet the structure and nature
of the society of the Tidewater is imprisoned in these
books in what Miss Glasgow once called, "a single luminous drop of experience."[43] And, although the "single
luminous drop" has a brief life span, the Tidewater society
is her subject and she describes it out of knowledge and
affection. Nevertheless, the mode she has chosen and the
style she has used become ultimately a thorough-going and
quite unsentimental attack upon the positive values of
the Tidewater South.

Miss Glasgow's ultimate position on this tradition and
on other Southern writers and their treatment of it is
ambivalent, however. The "comfortable mediocrity" which
constitutes for her the essence of "Americanism" she
deeply distrusts. The rebellion of the twentieth century
Southern writer is for her a source for praise, even while

she maintains serious reservations about the artistic and technical adequacy of the writers. "After breaking away from a petrified past overgrown by a funereal tradition," she says, "an impressive group of Southern writers recoiled from the uniform concrete surface of an industrialized South. . . . for the first time in its history, the South is producing, by some subtle process of aversion, a literature of revolt."[44] When she names some of the writers who are accomplishing this ideal, she includes Thomas Wolfe, William Faulkner, Allen Tate, and Caroline Gordon.

The Tidewater culture introduced into America the dream of the British aristocracy. It flourished in a dream of chivalric glory. The Tidewater and Low Country South gave order, leadership, and intellectual guidance to an agrarian culture. But, as Miss Glasgow demonstrates by personal example, by reiterated statement, and by dramatic presentation, it had reached the stage by the 1930's where its virtures were of the past, its strength in legends and not facts, and its structure honeycombed with the dry rot of time and custom. Not to love it was, for Miss Glasgow at least, impossible; and yet to fail to subject it to ironic analysis would be to succumb to its worst failings. Such a culture in such a state compellingly demanded to be treated in the novel of manners. Both it and we are fortunate that such a novelist was available as Ellen Glasgow.

THREE

William Faulkner:
The Anguished Dream of Time

> ... to write into them [the ledgers] the continuation
> of that record which two hundred years had not been
> enough to complete and another hundred would not
> be enough to discharge; that chronicle which was a
> whole land in miniature, which multiplied and com-
> pounded was the entire South ...
>
> *William Faulkner*[45]

BOTH THE TIDEWATER AND THE BACK-COUNTRY WERE ESTAB-
lished societies before the American Revolution, but the
third South, which we frequently call "The Deep South,"
came into being well after the establishment of the Federal
Union. It consists of western Georgia, western Tennessee,
Alabama, and Mississippi. (Louisiana with its French culture and its Spanish infusions is another, a different, and
a more difficult world, a Gallic society of Catholic leanings.) The Deep South was settled in substantial part by
the wild frontiersmen, whom W. J. Cash characterized as
"the half-wild Scotch and Irish clansmen of the seven-
teenth and eighteenth centuries,"[46] and by those who, for
various reasons of pride, failure, or crime, deserted the

Tidewater and the eastern portions of the Piedmont to leap over the mountain-South into a semi-tropical world and there to attempt to create, with all the distortions inherent in oral transmission and slow transportation, an order modeled on a partially understood dream of the Tidewater.

The region called at one time the Old Southwest represented the frontier in the 1830's and 1840's. In the 1820's it was almost untouched Indian territory. William Gilmore Simms, visiting his uncle and his father in 1824-1825 in Mississippi, was able to live among Indians and to travel great distances by horseback on a primitive frontier. When he returned to the same area in 1831, he found that the beginnings of a new culture had already been established and that, in small towns not unlike those that three decades later were to dot the trans-Mississippi Southwest, the white man was establishing a new social structure, and the Indian culture which at one time had dominated the region was passing away as the Indian found himself unable to survive the triple attacks of gunpowder, alcohol, and hordes of white men.[47]

During the "flush times" of the 1830's and 1840's in Mississippi and Alabama, many of the malcontents of the seaboard joined with the criminal and the displaced to transport a new culture to the region and began to develop towns, customs, and plantations, vaguely reminiscent of the ideal of Cavalier Virginia and Carolina. The importance of the Seaboard culture on the old Southwestern frontier resulted not so much from physical migration as from the transfer of a largely unrealized ideal. The plantation aristocrat was symbol, model, and goal for the ambitions of the frontiersman. That he was a model very imperfectly understood is the basis of one of the most tragic aspects of Southern history. Joseph Glover Baldwin writing back to Virginians about their fellow Virginians who had gone to this region could deal with amused detachment with the modifications which they made in the pattern of the dream of a landed aristocracy. His pieces in the *Southern Literary Messenger* are very much like the "Our Far-flung Correspondent" section of the *New Yorker* magazine today. When they were published in book form as *The Flush Times of Alabama and Mississippi* (1853), they became a record of the Tidewater's amused estimate of the raw frontier.

Here, too, the religious issue, which in the coastal tradition had been essentially that of an established church to which a gracious lip service was paid, was replaced not by the grim Calvinism and theologic earnestness of the Piedmont region but instead by a personal and extremely pietistic, superstitious kind of religion. The tradition of honor was realized not in graciousness of manner but in a code of violence; this view of honor carried a few hundred miles further west was to express itself in the sudden draw, the vigilante committee, and the individual gunman's assertion of his dignity with lead and gunpowder. In its earliest manifestations on the westward-moving frontier, it centered in the ostentatious standing-forth of an individual with flamboyant courage in the support of a code which was elaborate in its fine points and primitively exaggerated in its essential nature. This aspect of the Deep South Faulkner presents with great dramatic force in many places, of which "An Odor of Verbena" in *The Unvanquished* is a particularly clear example.

This harsh, violent, and exaggerated world was celebrated by the humorists of the old Southwest in books, sketches, and tales that in their own day were regarded as almost sub-literary but in our day have come to be seen as one of the major cultural manifestations of the region. Johnson Jones Hooper in *Some Adventures of Captain Simon Suggs, Late of the Tallapoosa Volunteers; Together* with *"Taking the Census"* and *Other Alabama Sketches* (1845) adopted the exaggerated tall tale and the extravagant act as typical of the region. The traditional Mike Fink material and Davy Crockett's *Autobiography* expressed a similar concept of an individual trying to carve out with great zest but also great difficulty a new way of life and one which appears to be a ridiculous posture to those who look at it with questioning, sophisticated eyes. This world has also proved in our time the subject for effective romantic treatment by writers like William Alexander Percy and Stark Young.

This Deep South William Faulkner made the subject of the bulk of his work. If the fragmentary segments of his long legend of Yoknapatawpha are put into a pattern, we see that his obsessive interest extends back into the remote days of the Chickasaw Indians who roamed the land, owned it, and lived under its trees and over its plains under a simple code of communal ownership. Faulkner pictures the coming of the white man, the introduction of a capitalistic system into a world with no previous sense of land ownership and the bringing by these white men of the Negro slave to do the labor. Thus there grew up in Mississippi, according to Faulkner's rather simplified and mythic treatment of the history of the Old Southwest, a peculiar culture that rested upon two great evil acts: the robbing of the displaced Red Man and the injustice done the Negro, whose labor, life, and blood were used as the raw materials for the building of estates and for the satisfaction of the concept of pride and honor on the part of men who saw wherever they turned the opportunity to carve out for themselves vast plantations, to attempt to realize grandiose dreams, and to build great dynasties.

In Faulkner's long record of this particular region and its history, he shows the building up of a code created by men of substantial but crude character and integrity, yet flawed by selfishness, by cruelty, and by slavery. The Civil War stands in Faulkner's world as the separating event in its history. Before it there was a society that had a peculiarly violent tradition of honor. After it there was decay, despair, and defeat. The remarkable thing is that these materials of the old Southwest, materials which had proved to be fruitful subjects for the literary comedians and which had been handled by them with detached amusement and by later local color writers with romantic sentimentality, became in William Faulkner's work the materials for transcendent romance and ultimately for great works of the imagination.

The ruling families—the Compsons, the McCaslins, and the others who dominated the region, and particularly the Sartorises, who seemed to stand for Faulkner's own family —after the Civil War had to exist in a world where the poor white, the under-privileged, and the ignorant joined hands with industrialism from the North and the West to force upon the entire region a modification of its social and economic system, a modification that was finally destructive of the virtues which it had created as well as the vices by which it had been sustained.

In Faulkner's fictive world, the members of these families act out great roles that are quite different from the actuality of the situations of their historical counterparts. If we view them with historical accuracy, we see that they are farmers, small shopkeepers, bankers, and political leaders of almost primitively small villages with a culture so rural and so "small-town" that its inhabitants are lost, bewildered, and ultimately betrayed whenever they step into a city of any size, whether it be New Orleans or Memphis. Yet Faulkner uses these figures as the substance for the retelling of the recurrent story of human dreams, bravery, and finally of defeat. He has elected to talk of them not realistically or humorously as their earlier chroniclers had dealt with them or with romantic appreciation as many other writers of this century have done but as the materials of what almost becomes a cosmic drama of history.

William Faulkner has worked in some very old tragic traditions. His attitudes toward his characters and the plots which he weaves around them seem to reach back to the early Greek drama and to primordial mythic patterns; so that his characters tend to become great symbolic beings, participating in actions that are intense, violent, and compulsive and which suggest Jung's racial unconscious. They loom larger than life. They become vast, almost phantasmagorial figures, outlined against grim skies and marching down long lanes of live oaks to vast white columns behind which are re-enacted the fate of the House of Atreus and the bloody deeds of Aeschylus's *Oresteia* trilogy. Thus he invests these people with noble roles and uses them to suggest something radically different from the realistic substance of the grubby lives which they literally live.

He has not only borrowed the relationships of characters and events from classic drama, he has also embedded them in plots that employ many of the characteristics of the traditional gothic novel and at the same time has remained keenly aware of the significance for these people of the psychological theories of Freud and Jung. He has also been a continual experimenter with the novel as a form, borrowing methods and techniques from James Joyce, Henry James, and other experimental writers and merging them in literary works of great surface complexity and intricacy of plot. He has adapted the stream-of-consciousness method to the problems of his legendary county so thoroughly that he is almost its only fully successful and truly original American practitioner.

He belongs, at the same time, to an older rhetorical tradition which emphasizes language and rhythm. In few American writers has a voice as distinctively his own as that of William Faulkner been heard; and to a remarkable degree this voice is present in all his works—even in those which appear, on the surface, at least, to be filtered through the minds, emotions, and words of characters in the novels.

The works which Faulkner has created about Yoknapa-tawpha County constitute thirteen separate volumes written between 1929 and 1962, plus a number of short stories which were published in magazines, then collected in separate volumes, and in 1950 were assembled under the title *Collected Stories.* Of the thirteen volumes independent of the *Collected Stories, The Unvanquished* (1938), *Go Down, Moses* (1942), and *Knight's Gambit* (1949) are collections of short stories and short novels that are only loosely woven together by their enveloping themes. The three books which make up the "Snopes Trilogy"—*The Hamlet* (1940), *The Town* (1957), and *The Mansion* (1959)—are loosely constructed novels weaving together a good deal of material that had earlier been written as short stories. Faulkner seemed to view his imaginary county and its history through individual characters and relatively limited actions. It seems as though Faulkner caught the people of his fictive world in a series of "strokes of the eye" which arrested their doomed flight in frozen moments of great significance and power. It has indeed been argued, though I must confess, unconvincingly to me, that Faulkner was not really able to handle the novel form but was primarily a writer who thought in terms of limited actions.[48] However, *The Sound and the Fury, As I Lay Dying, Light in August,* and *Absalom, Absalom!* are four novels of firm integrity and great strength. They appear to me to be not only unsurpassed in Faulkner's total career but also to constitute one of the major creations of the American imagination.

Among the sources and influences which Faulkner certainly felt in the creation of his novels and tales, in addition to Joyce and Sherwood Anderson, was a nineteenth century American tradition which included Hawthorne, Poe, and Melville, as Richard P. Adams has pointed out.[49] A number of people, among them Randall Stewart and William Van O'Connor,[50] have discussed the similarities between Nathaniel Hawthorne and Faulkner. The influence of Poe and his Gothic tradition on Faulkner's work also is clear. Mr. Adams suggests that *Absalom, Absalom!* might be called the "Fall of the House of Sutpen," because there are structural and thematic relationships which bind it to Poe's "Fall of the House of Usher." The influence of Melville has been less frequently suggested but still seems quite clear. On this point, Mr. Adams has an interesting and perhaps overly ingenious comparison of *Absalom, Absalom!* with *Moby Dick.* He says, "Sutpen, like Ahab, is a monomaniac, isolated by pride and suffering, 'wounded,' and seeking revenge by means of a ruthless exploitation of nature and other men; and like Ahab, he finally destroys himself and many of those around him because he tries to use and dominate, instead of participating in, the creative forces of love and fertility."[51] This observation, however unconvincing in its final state it may be, points persuasively to the tradition of American writing in which Faulkner belongs, the tradition of romantic symbolism. It is in George Snell's terms, and Faulkner's as well, "apocalyptic"[52] in that it uses exaggerated fables based upon reality in order to attempt to define a transcendent and cosmic order and a universal meaning.

To a certain extent, Faulkner's dealings with these materials followed the pattern of his own life. The Falkner family (William added the *u* to the spelling) was originally from Carolina. It migrated first to Tennessee where William C. Falkner, the novelist's great grandfather, was born in the 1820's. About 1840, this young Falkner left Tennessee, went to Mississippi, and established a home with his uncle, John Wesley Thompson, in Ripley, about fifty miles northeast of Oxford. The major families in Faulkner's imaginary history follow much the same pattern. The first of the McCaslins was born in Carolina in the 1770's and arrived in the second decade of the nineteenth century in Yoknapatawpha County bringing with him a wife, twin boys, and a daughter. Although he brought slaves with him from Carolina, the special and intricate inter-relationship of races and of families which the McCaslins established with their Negro slaves was a result of a special trip which he had made to New Orleans and on which he purchased a female slave named Eunice, who bore him a daughter named Tomey. This Tomey twenty years later became, through an incestuous relationship, the mother of another McCaslin known as Tomey's Turl. Hence, this early family brought from the Tidewater a tradition of plantations, attempted to build a great house and to establish a dynasty, and, through its inter-relationships with the Indians and with the Negroes, established that order upon a basic moral injustice.

Only a few years later the first of the Compsons came down the Natchez Trace to what was to become Jefferson; and there he built his house, his slave quarters, and his stable, and began the family which was for most of the nineteenth century to dominate a significant portion of the history of Yoknapatawpha County. Later in the century another newcomer, John Sartoris, also came from

Carolina bringing with him slaves and money and built his house just a few miles north of Jefferson.

Thus these great families established themselves in Yoknapatawpha County by moving from the coastal plantation tradition of Carolina and Virginia into the wilderness, there to carve out their own orders, to be caught in the dream of vast estates and great destinies. Each attempted, by his own lights, to create what Thomas Sutpen called his "design."

In actual fact, Yoknapatawpha is a county lacking in great wealth and in significant class distinctions. A man who rides into Yoknapatawpha in his formative years can ride out of nowhere and into nowhere in that pattern of solitary lonely movement which has been repeated over and over and over again as the American frontier has moved west. Irving Howe is probably right in saying that the basic social unit in Faulkner's imaginary world is not class but clan; and each of his major families comes finally to espouse a distinct kind of conduct which is based on the moral code of the clan. "It is through the breakup of the clans that Faulkner charts the decay of the traditional South," Mr. Howe suggests;[53] and although the three great clans—the Compsons, the Sartorises, and the McCaslins— begin as immigrants from the coast, acquire their land through the dispossession of the Chickasaw Indians, and build their estates through the efforts of the slaves, their histories after the Civil War begin to move in radically different patterns and indicate the kinds of response by which this dream of grandeur, however tawdrily realized, expresses itself in the face of defeat—the Sartorises, in recklessness and impetuous self-destruction; the Compsons, in the slow decay of will and of moral sense; the McCaslins, in the attempt to repudiate the guilt of the past and somehow to expiate its injustices.

While these families in their differing ways represent

the decay of a code, there grow up among them the Bundrens, the Tulls, the McCallons, the Armisteds, and finally the Snopeses, who come out of the impoverished and "poor white" group to achieve control of the modern world by embracing a course of action that is different from the code under which the "great" families lived.

This pattern is in a very literal sense an allegory woven imperfectly out of history. There are many different works in which it can be seen, but the most obvious of them all is *Absalom, Absalom!,* which certainly ranks high among Faulkner's major accomplishments and is, in Cleanth Brooks's opinion, which I share, one of the greatest and certainly the least well understood of Faulkner's novels.[54] If the view of the history of Yoknapatawpha as a sort of cosmic dream of history is to be taken seriously, then *Absalom, Absalom!* brings together more thoroughly and in a more compact form than any other of Faulkner's novels this particular sense of the past. Faulkner's materials are the native materials of his world, his own "postage stamp of earth" as it is expressed through the Southern myth, the Southern dream of its past, and the Southern memory.

The story of *Absalom, Absalom!* deals with this area in an extremely complex and confused manner. Indeed, the term "anti-narrative" has been used to describe it. Its central plot is extremely complex, but the way in which that plot is revealed is even more complicated. There is, perhaps, no other novel of major stature by an American which leaves as many of its basic questions to the reader's own judgment as *Absalom, Absalom!* does. It contains at its end a Chronology in which the events of the story are set down, a Genealogy in which the characters of the story are described in terms of their inter-relationship with other characters, and the famous map of Jefferson, Yoknapatawpha County, Mississippi, "William Faulkner,

Sole Owner and Proprietor."⁵⁵ Yet these materials are less
than fully adequate for the explication of the story.
Cleanth Brooks has done us all a yeoman service in setting
down what the various narrators of the story know and do
not know about the events of the novel and in making a
list of the most important conjectures which are advanced
by its various narrators. This list of conjectures covers
great segments of the story and constitutes five and one-
half pages of closely printed data in Mr. Brooks's magnificent *William Faulkner: The Yoknapatawpha Country.*
The plot of the story quite plainly is not easy to come by.

    In the broadest outline, it is somewhat like this: Thomas
Sutpen was born in the mountains of what is now West
Virginia in 1807. He is defined by his creator as being
one of several children of "poor whites of Scotch-English
stock."⁵⁶ Thus his origins are in the Piedmont South.
When he was in his early teens, his family moved to Tidewater Virginia; and there for the first time, he came in
contact with the plantation system. He belonged himself
to a region and class "where what few other people he
knew lived in log cabins boiling with children like the
one he was born in—men and grown boys who hunted or
lay before the fire on the floor while the women and older
girls stepped back and forth across them to reach the fire
to cook, where the only colored people were Indians and
you only looked down at them over your rifle sights, where
he had never heard of, never imagined, a place, a land
divided neatly up and actually owned by men who did
nothing but ride over it on fine horses or sit in fine clothes
on the galleries of big houses while other people worked
for them; he did not even imagine then that there was any
such way to live or to want to live, or that there existed all
the objects to be wanted which there were, or the ones
who owned the objects not only could look down on the
ones that didn't, but could be supported in the down-

looking not only by the others who owned objects too but
by the very ones that were looked down on that didn't
own objects and knew they never would. Because where he
lived the land belonged to anybody and everybody and so
the man who would go to the trouble and work to fence
off a piece of it and say 'This is mine' was crazy."[57]

This boy, out of an innocence which did not let him
know that distinctions among men could rest on anything
other than their luck, which denied any intrinsic differences among men, came at last to see the ordered society
which the Tidewater represented; and there "because he
had not only not lost the innocence yet, he had not yet
discovered that he possessed it. He no more envied the
man [who owned a plantation] than he would have envied
a mountain man who happened to own a fine rifle. He
would have coveted the rifle, but he would himself have
supported and confirmed the owner's pride and pleasure
in its ownership because he could not have conceived of
the owner taking such crass advantage of the luck which
gave the rifle to him rather than another as to say to other
men: *Because I own this rifle, my arms and legs and blood
and bones are superior to yours.*"[58] Sent to one of the
great houses in the Tidewater, Sutpen was met at the door
by a Negro servant who instructed him that he could not
enter and told him to go to the back door. He thus received a trauma resulting from his innocence being destroyed through the recognition that birth, blood, and
family could give distinctions independent of strength or
skill or luck.

Having seen this new world of caste and class, he embarked upon what he called "his grand design" to establish
for himself a mansion such as that from which he had been
turned away. He went first to the West Indies and there
rose to a position of power, married and had a son, only
to discover after the birth of the son that there was Negro

blood in the woman whom he had married. He put her and the child aside and came in 1833 into Jefferson, Mississippi, where he acquired a hundred square miles of bottom land from a Chickasaw chief, paying out his last money to record the deed. Later he returned with a wagon load of Negroes and a French architect and drove them to wrench out of the wilderness itself a vast mansion designed by the architect and executed by the Negro slaves. Then Sutpen married Ellen Coldfield, the daughter of a pious man and storekeeper, and thus attempted to achieve some stability and respectability.

He had two children, Henry and Judith. Henry he sent to the University of Mississippi when it was a backwoods school; and there Henry met Charles Bon, ten years older, who had come from New Orleans to attend the University of Mississippi and who was, in fact, the child of Sutpen's West Indian wife. At the outbreak of the Civil War, the triangle played itself out. Sutpen, his son Henry, and his son Charles, who now was in love with and wished to marry Judith Sutpen, all went off to war; and when at last the war was over, Henry and Charles came back to Sutpen's Hundred; and, to prevent Charles's marrying their sister Judith, Henry shot Charles at the plantation gate and disappeared. Sutpen returning from the war found his dream of a dynastic order in ruins, his wife dead some three years, one son murdered by another who was now a fugitive, and his daughter confirmed in her refusal to marry anyone.

In order to secure a male heir, he suggested to his sister-in-law, Rosa Coldfield, that if they could produce a child and it were a boy and it lived that he would marry her. She indignantly refused; and Sutpen then seduced the fifteen-year-old Milly Jones, daughter of Wash Jones, who had been his "poor white" handy man and occasional drinking companion; but Milly's child was a daughter;

and Sutpen disowned her and the child on the day of its birth. Wash Jones in revenge took a scythe and destroyed Sutpen and killed the daughter and the infant. Judith went on living in the plantation house with her closest companion, her half-Negro sister, Clytemnestra. She sent to New Orleans and brought back Charles Étienne de Saint-Valery Bon who had been Charles's child by his octoroon mistress; and Judith and Clytie raised the boy who appeared to be white but who finally rejected his claim on whiteness and married a very black and ape-like Negro woman who bore him an idiot son named Jim Bond. Étienne died of yellow fever; Judith came down with the disease while she was nursing him and also died.

In 1909 Miss Rosa Coldfield found that there was some-one other than Clytie and the idiot Jim Bond living in the dilapidated old house at Sutpen's Hundred, and accom-panied by Quentin Compson, she went out to investigate. There she found Henry Sutpen in hiding, ill, but cared for by Clytie. Three months later Miss Rosa brought an ambulance to take Henry to the hospital; but Clytie, thinking that Henry was being taken to be punished for killing Charles almost fifty years before, set fire to the house and burned it down, destroying herself and Henry; and the only remaining fragment of Thomas Sutpen's dream was an idiot Negro grandson, Jim Bond, who wan-dered howling through the ashes of the ruined mansion. However inaccurate his view of history may be, Faulkner in this novel ties together in a single dramatic action the three Souths in a peculiar and historically effective rela-tionship.

Yet the most difficult portion of this complex story lies not in its gothic dramatic plot but in the fact that it is told by a group of people none of whom really knows what takes place. The first of these narrators is Miss Rosa Cold-field, to whom Sutpen is a devil incarnate. A second narrator is the father of Quentin Compson, who knows primarily what he learned from General Compson, Quentin's grandfather. Through him the town's view of Sutpen is presented—as a man recovering from a recent illness, owning little but his guns and his horse, and attempting to carve out a position for himself in an unfriendly society. Much of the narrative takes place in the college dormitory room at Harvard where Quentin Compson and his roommate Shreve McCannon attempt to reconstruct the story, to dramatize in their own minds the events which lead up to its various crises, and to conclude that somehow or other this narrative represents an embodiment of the entire South.

The outside viewer, Shreve, half amused that these fantastic figures should assume their place upon a stage as vast as that which Quentin gives them, finally sums the story up in these matter-of-fact terms: "So it took Charles Bon and his mother to get rid of old Tom, and Charles Bon and the octoroon to get rid of Judith, and Charles Bon and Clytie to get rid of Henry; and Charles Bon's mother and Charles Bon's grandmother got rid of Charles Bon. So it takes two niggers to get rid of one Sutpen."[59] On the other hand, the surviving Jim Bond becomes for Shreve a symbol of the South and its future. However, Quentin is unable to accept this view of the world.

None of these actions are ever at the center of the stage; but the narrators in their differings ways, sharing and commenting and speculating about their various ignorances, conduct a kind of public inquiry in the year 1909, reviewing through hearsay the events of these vast and shadowy figures from their own past. They are quite close in nature and in function to the Chorus in a Greek tragedy. Their speculative and philosophical discourse not only invests the characters with special magnitude, it forms an incomplete dialectical commentary, which forms a special drama of narration. Thus Sutpen, Judith, Henry, Charles Bon, the "grand design," the vast mansion molded from the mud of Sutpen's Hundred, the Civil War, and the impact which it has upon those who are caught in it—all become dramatically represented not through their own actions but through the impressions which they create on later generations.

Sutpen, Faulkner has emphatically declared, is the central character in *Absalom, Absalom!*. Faulkner described the novel in these terms in an interview at the University of Virginia: "The story of a man who wanted a son and got too many, got so many that they destroyed him. It's incidentally the story of Quentin Compson's hatred of the bad qualities in the country he loves. But the central character is Sutpen, the story of a man who wanted sons."[60] Asked if the Civil War was the cause for Sutpen's downfall, Mr. Faulkner said that it was not, that he had "used the Civil War" for his own purposes, that Sutpen's destruction was a function of his own character, and that Sutpen was finally killed by a very obvious example of the "poor white" who was, according to Faulkner's statement of intention, a conscious representation of historical fact.[61] He said, "Wash Jones represented the man who survived the Civil War. The aristocrat in the columned house was ruined but Wash Jones survived it unchanged."[62] Attempting to describe once what he intended as Sutpen's central characteristic, Faulkner said, "To me he is to be pitied. He was not depraved—he was amoral, he was ruthless, completely self-centered. To me he is to be pitied, as anyone who ignores man is to be pitied, who does not believe that he belongs as a member of a human family, of the human family, is to be pitied."[63]

Commenting on the method by which he composed

Absalom, Absalom!, through the voices of people who knew the story only partially, Faulkner said, "No one individual can look at truth. It blinds you. You look at it and you see one phase of it. Someone else looks at it and sees a slightly awry phase of it. But taken all together, the truth is in what they saw though nobody saw the truth intact. So these are true as far as Miss Rosa and as Quentin saw it. Quentin's father saw what he believed was truth, that was all he saw. But the old man was himself a little too big for people no greater in stature than Quentin and Miss Rosa and Mr. Compson to see all at once. It would have taken a wiser or more tolerant or more sensitive or more thoughtful person to see him as he was. It was . . . thirteen ways of looking at a blackbird. But the truth, I would like to think, comes out, that when the reader has read all these thirteen different ways of looking at the blackbird, the reader has his own fourteenth image of that blackbird which I would like to think is the truth."[64]

That Faulkner in this novel was consciously thinking of the old Greek concept of man became clear when he was asked what it was that destroyed Sutpen. He said, "The Greeks destroyed him, the old Greek concept of tragedy. He wanted a son which symbolized this ideal, and he got too many sons—his sons destroyed one another and then him. He was left with—the only son he had left was a Negro."[65]

I am not attempting here to arrive at this fourteenth way of looking at a blackbird but to suggest that a writer who views his materials in this way and presents them through such dramatic representation and then wraps the story up in as complex a pattern of rhetoric and evocative language as Faulkner does is working in a tradition that is different from that of Ellen Glasgow, that of the Tidewater, that of the novel of manners. Only a reader without an ear could imagine Ellen Glasgow writing a sentence such as this: "I, the dreamer clinging yet to the dream as a patient clings to the last thin unbearable, ecstatic instant of agony in order to sharpen the sabre of the pain's surcease, waking into the reality, the more than reality, not to the unchanged and unaltered old time but into a time altered to fit the dream which, conjunctive with the dreamer, becomes immolated and apotheosized."[66] And it is almost equally difficult to imagine Thomas Wolfe writing such a sentence.

For Faulkner the transmontane attempt to recreate the Tidewater dream becomes a record of the peculiar social institutions which he knows. Certainly he is trying to relate the things which he has to say to the South about which he says them. He replied to a question about whether he meant the relationship between Charles Bon and Sutpen to be parallel to the general racial situation in the South with this remark, "It was a manifestation of the general racial system in the South which was condensed and concentrated as the writer has got to do with any incident or any character he takes, for the reason that he hasn't got sixty years. He has got to do his job in—between the covers of a book, but—that is, epitomize a constant general condition in the South, yes."[67] Thus one of Faulkner's modes, the apocalyptic mode, is made to serve his sense of the region and the various Souths. His methods of convoluted and emotion-charged prose, rich with the quality of oratory, incantatory in the way in which he plays with words almost independent of meaning so that out of them emerges not a clear statement of fact but an aura of feeling—this method which in Faulkner's hands was employed with great effectiveness in *Absalom, Absalom!* and in his other and best novels comes close to transcending the materials of his world. Its use makes of his works a cosmic drama and represents a mode in Southern fiction which in our time has attracted the attention not only of literary critics and readers in this country but in the world at large.

There can be little question about the intensity of the response which Faulkner gives to the materials of his world. There can be, and there is, much question remaining as to whether or not the tremendous emotional response which we today are giving to Faulkner's work is a response which still will be present when the immediate social issues with which it deals—those of race and class—have passed into a different phase and when the work must survive not in terms of what is happening today in Mississippi or in Alabama but in terms of how these historical data have been used to make a statement about the remote past and to use that statement to talk of man's lot in his world. Faulkner's rural world is one of small men, small planters, small businessmen; but he has invested these men with an intense response, with a search for meaning, with a cataclysmic energy so that they loom larger than life and become overwhelmingly representative of ideas and of regions, and some of that energy is borrowed from the present day historical context. Such a method runs a grave risk. As Hemingway indicated in *Death in the Afternoon,* "In writing for a newspaper you told what happened and . . . you communicated the emotion aided by the element of timeliness which gives a certain emotion to any account of something that has happened on that day."[68] In our time, when the issue of race is world-wide and powerfully evocative, who can say what amount of Faulkner's power is borrowed from our present difficulties?

At the heart of what Faulkner does is the historical myth which is most plainly told in Thomas Sutpen's story. None of the characters that tell it know quite what it means, and different aspects of it fascinate each of them. And this is, I think, true for the reader, as, I suspect, it must have been for Mr. Faulkner himself. Sutpen in *Absalom, Absalom!* meant something about the history of the South. Just what, none of us know; but that the history of the South is a microcosm of the whole macrocosmic nature of human experience Faulkner feels certain. I share his certainty and will be surprised if this cosmic meaning does not transcend the passing of the emotions inherent in the events he uses.

FOUR

Thomas Wolfe:
The Epic of the National Self

> . . . every man on earth held in the little tenement
> of his flesh and spirit the whole ocean of human life
> and time. . . .
>
> *Thomas Wolfe*[69]

BOTH THE SOUTHERN SEABOARD AND THE DEEP SOUTH WERE
haunted by the dream of Baronial splendor. As a powerful
dream, it realized itself in a mannered but intense code of
violence in the Gulf Plain states. Whatever limited reality
it had came from the Seaboard planter world. But behind
the Tidewater and the Low Country was a world of sturdy,
egalitarian men who settled and dominated the westward
sweep of continent beyond the "fall-line." The piedmont
hills, the mountain ranges, and the mountain valleys were
first colonized primarily not by the British with Cavalier
pretentions, who entered through the Southern Atlantic
ports and then moved inward, but by those of Scotch-Irish,
Scottish, and German origin who came through the middle
Atlantic ports of Philadelphia, Chester, and New Castle,
and moved westward through the Great Valley for about
a hundred miles until the tall mountains raised barriers that

49

deflected them south. They came down the broad cattle trails into the Piedmont South settling in Virginia, the backcountry of the Carolinas, Tennessee, and Georgia. There they created a social world marked by the grim Calvinistic attitudes of the dour Scottish Presbyterians and took unto themselves the piedmont and mountain regions stretching from what is now West Virginia to a point in central and south Georgia.

When the "Great Migration" of the Scotch-Irish began in 1717, few of the migrants questioned the propriety of social classes or the value of a society with stability based on a concept of upper, "middling," and "lower" orders. But in America, particularly in mountainous Virginia and the backcountry of the Carolinas, class lines were soon blurred almost beyond recognition and traditional distinctions underwent massive erosion. These people of the Piedmont created a special and frequently grim way of life so radically different from the Tidewater culture, which was only a few hundred miles away, that they might almost have lived on different continents. In this grim social world of the frontier Piedmont, the Scotch-Irish were quick-tempered, impetuous, inclined to work by fits and starts, reckless, and given to too much drinking. Their pietistic, puritanic Calvinism was yoked to an intense acquisitiveness, so that they earned the claim that a "Scotch-Irishman is one who keeps the commandments of God and every other thing he can get his hands on." Thus they formed a harsh society marked by widespread crudity and high animal spirits. It was an egalitarian, individualistic, religiously dissenting world. To those who visited it from the coastal plain area, it appeared to be lawless and frightening. The Anglican itinerate minister Charles Woodmason, who tried to serve the South Carolina backcountry from 1766 to 1768, left in his *Journal* a record of the dismay with which he viewed the region. He declared that these people's chief characteristics were lawlessness, vile manners, ignorance, slovenliness, and primitive emotionalism in religion.

Their pragmatic view of life, their folk-version Calvinism, and their anti-intellectual individualism created a special world favorable to egalitarian democracy and having little patience with and no respect for aristocratic pretensions. This cotton country and hill country, made up of small farms, small towns, and small cities spaced very far apart, maintains to this day many of its early characteristics.

It is very far removed from the melancholy great oaks and broad plantations of the Tidewater and almost equally removed from the tropical lushness and richness of the Deep South. Here in the decades immediately before the Revolution was the sharp cutting edge of the frontier. Although by 1790 the Scotch-Irish represented no more than a quarter of a million Americans, their strength of character shaped the conventions of the world in which they lived and made them the controlling force for awhile in the westward movement. It was and is a country at the mercy of the capriciousness of weather and the vicissitudes of the cotton market. In this century it has been a land racked by diseases peculiar to poverty, a harsh sharecropper system, and by low income and little education. It is no accident that this area has been a central target for a war on poverty and economic and social distress by a socially-minded Federal government from the early days of Franklin D. Roosevelt's presidency to the present programs of Lyndon B. Johnson.

There has not been a time since the eighteenth century when this Piedmont and Mountain South has not had its chroniclers, and its recorders have had a remarkable unanimity of opinion and attitude toward its inhabitants. The most obvious characteristic of this body of writers, aside from their exaggerated tendency toward the grotesque, is an emphasis upon a disordered society, a sense that there is neither in social custom nor in religious belief an ordering principle which is acceptable to the writer. As early as 1728, William Byrd in his *A History of the Dividing Line* portrayed backcountry North Carolinians, whom he called the inhabitants of "lubberland," with an amused awareness that at least by his standards they were grotesques. Augustus Baldwin Longstreet described the people of the Georgia Piedmont in a series of sketches written in the 1830's and collected in book form in 1835 as *Georgia Scenes.* His is the detached view of a cultivated lawyer and judge viewing these people as cruel and unlearned denizens of a world remote from the social order which Judge Longstreet revered.

The early novels about the Southern frontier described the same kinds of people and judged them against a concept of an aristocratic social order, notably in the case of William Gilmore Simm's "Border Romances" and most obviously in his *Guy Rivers* (1834), which is laid in frontier Georgia. In the mid-century George Washington Harris in his comic character Sut Lovingood created a kind of American *Til Eulenspiegel* in this region. During the Local Color Movement writers like "Charles Egbert Craddock" (Mary N. Murphree) presented a whimsical picture with a summer visitor's condescension of the eccentricities of the mountain people of this region.

In the twentieth century the region has called forth notable novelistic efforts, among them the works of T. S. Stribling, particularly in *Teeftallow* and in his trilogy *The Forge, The Store,* and *The Unfinished Cathedral;* Erskine Caldwell, in his earlier and more serious time when his Rabelaisian exaggeration was redeemed from vulgarity by his social anger; Lillian Smith, in her tractarian novels and essays; and most recently Flannery O'Connor, whose two novels and two volumes of short stories may very well represent the best writing done by a Southerner during the past fifteen years.

The writers of this tradition used many different literary forms. They have, however, all sought in differing ways for some outside, some external control by which they can judge the value of the society which they discuss. This society is in many ways more nearly American and less distinctively Southern, except for its grotesquerie, than the societies of the Deep South or of the Tidewater and the Low Country; and the standard by which it is judged, whether it be that of social justice, of religious order, or of moral indignation, has always been an outer and different standard from that embraced by the local inhabitants. Ellen Glasgow and William Faulkner, on the other hand, have found the standards by which to judge their societies in the ideals of their citizens, however little these ideals found firm expression in either of the cultures.

Many of the writers who deal with the Piedmont South, including Thomas Wolfe, launch attacks upon its impoverished culture much like those made by the middle-western writers who participated in "The Revolt from the Village"—writers like E. W. Howe, Joseph Kirkland, Hamlin Garland, and Sinclair Lewis, who was a major influence on Thomas Wolfe's work. As early as 1923 Wolfe had written to his mother contemptuously of "those people who shout 'Progress, Progress, Progress'—when what they mean is more Ford automobiles, more Rotary Clubs, more Baptist Ladies Social Unions."[70] Here, as it is in the works of Lewis, the author's anger is directed at Main Street and Booster's Clubs, at a kind of "village virus" which was neither regional nor national, but the product of blatant commercialism and ugliness, of the worship of size and glitter wherever they might be found.

Where Ellen Glasgow used the novel of manners and

William Faulkner the symbolic romance to give their fictional representations of their Souths, Thomas Wolfe turned to a kind of fiction which was lyric rather than dramatic, which was characterized by autobiographical plots rather than by tight structures, and which dealt with the problem of the definition of the self in relation first to a middle-class Piedmont South and later to the great world outside the region. The South which Wolfe knew was consciously Roundhead in its political allegiance, strongly egalitarian and individualistic in its view of man, characterized by rough, coarse, crude, and graceless manners and conventions, and grimly Calvinistic in its religious orientation.

In this respect, Thomas Wolfe takes his place very clearly and plainly as a writer about a South that is significantly different from that which we had seen before. That Wolfe knew that his world was a different one from that of many other Southerners he made very clear. In *The Web and the Rock,* he contrasts two sections of the South in terms of "Old Catawba" and South Carolina, where "Old Catawba" is very plainly piedmont North Carolina. In making this distinction, he echoes that old, old remark that North Carolina is a vale of humility between two mountains of conceit. He says, "Old Catawba has the slants of evening and the mountain cool. You feel lonely in Old Catawba, but it is not the loneliness of South Carolina. In Old Catawba, the hill boy helps his father building fences and hears a soft Spring howling in the wind, and sees the wind snake through the bending waves of the coarse grasses of the mountain pastures. And far away he hears the whistle's cry wailed back, far-flung and faint along some mountain valley, as a great train rushes toward the cities of the East. And the heart of the hill boy will know joy because he knows, all world-remote, lonely as he is, that some day he will meet the world and know those cities too."[71]

Against that sense of difference and of outward movement, Wolfe poses a view of South Carolina that is far from complimentary. "These people," he says, "are really lost. They cannot get away from South Carolina, and if they get away they are no good. They drawl beautifully. There is the most wonderful warmth, affection, heartiness in their approach and greeting, but the people are afraid. Their eyes are desperately afraid, filled with a kind of tortured and envenomed terror of the old, stricken, wounded 'Southness' of cruelty and lust. Sometimes their women have the honey skins, they are like gold and longing. They are filled with the most luscious and seductive sweetness, tenderness, and gentle mercy. But the men are stricken. They get fat about the bellies, or they have a starved, stricken leanness in the loins."[72]

Such a distinction Wolfe pushes beyond the limits of reality. The difference between South Carolina and North Carolina is far less than it is indicated as being here; but he sees all of North Carolina in terms of his own mountain and piedmont region and all South Carolina in terms of the Low Country society. He declares, "Old Catawba is a place inhabited by humble people. There is no Charleston in Old Catawba, and not so many people pretending to be what they are not. . . . Now their pretense is reduced to pretending that they amounted to so much formerly. And they really amounted to very little."[73] Yet Wolfe knows, too, that "Old Catawba" is not of a piece. In *The Web and The Rock*, he says: "Down in the East, in Old Catawba, they have some smack of ancientry. The East got settled first and there are a few old towns down there, the remnants of plantations, a few fine old houses, a lot of niggers, tobacco, turpentine, pine woods, and the mournful flat-lands of the coastal plain. The people in the East used to think they were better than the people in the West because they had been there a little longer. But they were not really better. In the West, where the mountains sweep around them, the people have utterly common, familiar, plain, Scotch-Irish faces, and names like Weaver, Wilson, Gudger, Joyner, Alexander, and Patton. The West is really better than the East. . . . The West is really a region of good small people, a Scotch-Irish place, and that, too, is undefined, save that it doesn't drawl so much, works harder, doesn't loaf so much, and shoots a little straighter when it has to. It is really just one of the common places of the earth, a million or two people with nothing very extraordinary about them."[74] Thus Wolfe's attitude toward his region is ambiguous; for, while he is highly critical of the crass materialism of the Piedmont, he also loves it and finds it better than the Tidewater.

Certainly Wolfe does not embrace the concept of the nobility of the Old South. Even in his early plays such as *Mannerhouse* and *The Mountain,* Wolfe dealt in unfriendly and destructive ways with the legend of the aristocratic South. His third long play *Welcome to Our City* is also an attack on the social conventions and beliefs of his own region. This quality in Wolfe's work led his Chapel Hill classmate, Jonathan Daniels, in reviewing *Look Homeward Angel* to declare that in that book "North Carolina and the South are spat upon." Such critical attitudes are not surprising about a writer in the tradition within which Wolfe grew up. Freed from the deep emotional commitment typical of the Tidewater and the Deep South, Wolfe could look calmly and critically at his region, deplore its weaknesses, and love its strengths, without indulging in the emotional upheaval over this ambivalent attitude which Quentin Compson suffers in *Absalom, Absalom!.* The tendency of Faulkner and Miss Glasgow in their differing ways is to have as a subject a social order which serves as a frame within which they may describe their characters, so that the region and its history, the people and their customs, ultimately work upon the individual characters in their books at the same time that they are created by these characters. Thus a complex and subtle interrelationship between character and region emerges from their studies. On the other hand, for Wolfe no such firm structure of society existed; and he turned, as Whitman had earlier turned, and as de Tocqueville had suggested that the American democratic artist must always turn, from the egalitarian social world to the inner self for the true subject of his work.

The South which Wolfe lived in as a boy and young man he saw as an entangling web to be broken through in the effort toward self-realization. The past makes no compulsive demands upon him, for Thomas Wolfe is fleeing the hills relatively unencumbered by history, looking back at the past not in love or pain but in anger, and finally turning, like Eugene Gant at the end of *Look Homeward Angel*, ". . . like a man who stands upon a hill above the town he has left, yet does not say, 'The town is near,' but turns his eyes upon the distant soaring ranges."[75] These ranges not only were geographically but spiritually to the North and West. Thus Wolfe becomes relatively free of his past—the first Southern American writer of major stature who deserts his region to embrace a national and then an international identity. Though he has a firm sense of the social world he is leaving, the center of his books is not that social world but himself; and like Alexis de Tocqueville's American of 1831, he finds that the only adequate subject for the democratic writer is himself. De Tocqueville says: "Among a democratic people poetry will not be fed with legends or the memorials of old traditions. . . . All these resources fail him; but Man remains, and the poet needs no more. The destinies of mankind, man himself taken aloof from his country and his age and standing in the presence of Nature and of God, with his passions, his doubts, his rare prosperities and inconceivable wretchedness, will become the chief, if not the sole, theme of poetry among these nations."[76] In a sense, what de Tocqueville is suggesting is that the absence of formal caste systems and of a formal pattern of manners renders democratic writers helpless in the presentation of those aspects of society outside the individual. He is repeating what James Fenimore Cooper had earlier expressed as the American "poverty of materials." Cooper enumerates the things that are missing as "no annals for the historian; no follies (beyond the most vulgar and commonplace) for the satirist; no manners for the dramatist; no obscure fictions for the writer of romance. . . ."[77] In a sense de Tocqueville and Cooper defined a problem more real for the Middle Atlantic states than it was for a region which owed its allegiance, however unrealistically, to a traditional order, a pattern of polite manners, and a society with sharply defined hierarchal levels.

Although Wolfe was of the South and like Quentin Compson both loved and hated it, he regarded himself as more American than Southern, and he embraced the epic and lyric traditions rather than the realistic or apocalyptic ones. In every great age of a national or racial culture, there have been writers who have felt among their deepest compulsions the urge to give expression to the national spirit; and the genre which they have chosen most often has been that of the epic. Through the epic hero they have tried to express the highest ideals of their age. John Crowe Ransom said, ". . . the epic arises as the expression of a nation which has gone through its strife. And it is the representation of the struggle to maintain its ideals and to express its religion and its culture and its heroism."[78]

The characteristic spirit of America has been that of an egalitarian man. In its ideal state it is a nation in which the old hierarchal systems, the old classes, the complex structures of protocol, of rank, and of birth have been erased; and in their stead stands the individual at the center of the human scheme not because he differs from his fellows but because he sums them up, and this individual is at the heart of the national spirit not because he is better than those around him but because they are no better than he. This notion of equality, as potent as any ideal released from the mind of man, found in the American wilderness, in its towering mountains and its vast plains, in its valleys, villages, and growing towns an area within which man can test his potentiality to build a better world; and it is through the struggle of this common man to create a world which has special meaning that the human imagination was given a new dimension by the American experience and had to find somehow a means of creating a hero who embodies the unique spirit of his time and place and is a man representative of the democratic masses.

The American attempting to create this epic hero has been forced finally to the realization that for him, as it had been for Henry David Thoreau, the only subject which he knew well enough and which had significance enough for artistic expression was himself. As Emerson suggested, perhaps inaccurately, "Dante's praise is that he dared to write his autobiography in colossal cipher, or into universality."[79] This view of the self is in one sense an answer to two strong counter-pulls in American life. One is the strong pull toward the building of a good and democratic society, toward creating in the new world an equitable social order "with liberty and justice for all." The other pull is the premium which the ideal of absolute equality places upon the individual and upon his self-realization. This proud, active, lonely, and self-contained figure has become in our imagination the mythic American. From James Fenimore Cooper to Gary Cooper and the T. V. Western, this nameless American rides out of nowhere—rootless, alone, and "Westering"— for awhile resolves a situation, only at last to ride once more and forever into the western sunset, homeless, active, and larger than life, his shadow falling behind him as the light fades from the vast and cruel sky. It is in his effort to describe this kind of American and to satisfy this sort of condition and to define this peculiarly American loneliness that Thomas Wolfe worked.

Look Homeward, Angel, Wolfe's first book, is the record of the growth of a child from his birth until his college education is completed. It places a very great premium upon the impact on its protagonist, Eugene Gant, of the physical world, the social structure, and the actions of individual friends and acquaintances. In a style richly poetic and strongly evocative, Wolfe traces here the experiences of a delicate boy struggling to know himself in "the limitless meadows of sensation." But this boy, by Wolfe's own definition, is unique only in the degree of his sensitivity, not in his basic nature. "Each of us," he declares in the opening of the book, "is all the sums he has not counted; subtract us into nakedness and night again, and you shall see begin in Crete four thousand years ago the love that ended yesterday in Texas. . . . Each moment is the fruit of forty thousand years. The minute-winning days, like flies, buzz home to death, and every moment is a window on all time."[80]

It is in the spirit of this generic man that Wolfe defines the lonely search of his characters, the search for communion, the search for meaning, the search for the deepest nature of the self, the old Wordsworthian search backward into the individual's origins in order to find the nature and meaning of the self. In the Prologue to *Look Homeward, Angel,* Wolfe sees himself and others as "in exile," sees our world as "the unspeakable and incommunicable prison," and declares, "Remembering speechlessly we seek the great forgotten language, the lost lane-end into heaven, a stone, a leaf, an unfound door."[81]

When Eugene Gant moves from Altamont, a thinly disguised equivalent of Asheville, and from Pulpit Hill, an even more thinly disguised equivalent of Chapel Hill, he moves outward into the great world; and though he takes with him many of the qualities which he sees as the virtues of the South, he consciously leaves his native region for what he believes to be a better world. In *The Web and the Rock* Wolfe's protagonist remembers "all the times when he had come out of the South and into the North, and always the feeling was the same—an exact, pointed, physical feeling marking the frontiers of his consciousness with a geographic precision. . . . It was a geographic division of the spirit that was sharply, physically exact, as if it had been cleanly severed by a sword. . . . He ducked his head a little as if he were passing through a web. He knew that he was leaving the South . . . Every young man from the South has felt this precise and formal geography of the spirit."[82] Certainly Wolfe is not right in attributing to all Southerners that sense of expansion and release which crossing the Potomac gives him. Indeed, that kind of release is something which neither Ellen Glasgow nor William Faulkner would have wanted or would have expressed.

Of Time and the River, Wolfe's longest and most diffuse book, carries his protagonist from Altamont to Harvard, then to New York City, and finally to Europe. Eugene Gant experiences in this steadily outward movement an increasing necessity to describe and to define himself, not as a Southerner but as an American and to

begin a roll call of names and places which includes the
South as simply a part of the larger world but does not
isolate it as a unique subject. Typically in his catalogues—
close in content and cadence to those of Walt Whitman—
are lists of names such as he gives in one place in *Of
Time and the River* where he names "The Wilderness;
and the names of Antietam, Chancellorsville, Shiloh, Bull
Run, Fredericksburg, Cold Harbor . . . Cowpens, Brandy-
wine, and Saratoga; of Death Valley, Chickamauga, and
the Cumberland Gap. The names of the Nantahalahs, the
Bad Lands, the Painted Desert, the Yosemite, and the
Little Big Horn; the names of Yancey and Cabarrus coun-
ties; and the terrible names of Hatteras." The significance
of such a catalogue is its indiscriminate inclusiveness, just
as his "continental thunder of the states" begins with
"Montana, Texas, Arizona, Colorado, Michigan, Mary-
land, Virginia, and the two Dakotas."[83] Such catalogues
are recurrent in Wolfe—he lists the names of Indian tribes,
of railways, of hoboes, of great rivers, and his listing does
not end in America but goes on to the Tiber and the
Thames. Wolfe's characters through their absorption of
great ranges of experience and their merging of myriad
persons with themselves become archetypes of the American.

In *The Web and the Rock* Wolfe returns to the same
story with a new protagonist; and he repeats many of the
incidents of the earlier work in recounting the experience
of George Webber whose record begins when he is a child
in Libya Hill, another thin disguise for Asheville, and who
moves on out into the larger world of the North and of
Europe. In *You Can't Go Home Again*, George Webber
returns briefly to the South, writes a novel, travels in
England and on the continent, and experiences both directly and vicariously the "complex fate" of being an
American. At the conclusion of this collection of materials

—which are so loosely organized that the book can hardly be called a novel in any strict sense of the term—Webber gives an emphatic expression to a nationally oriented sense of democracy and its promise.

In *You Can't Go Home Again,* Webber sees people and actions more frequently than he participates in events, and the forms in which he sees them are often virtually self-contained units of the length of tales and novellas. Indeed, as it did for Faulkner, experience very often came to Wolfe in actions which were friendly to representation in short stories and short novels. After *Look Homeward, Angel,* which is itself an uneven book, Wolfe did not again produce a work in which the individual episodes are not more impressive than the whole of which they are a part. Both Faulkner and Wolfe attempted to formulate large structures which adequately controlled and shaped the individual dramatic scenes and in which their works appear naturally to fall. Faulkner chose the historical and social history of his region and used it to reflect universal experience. Wolfe, on the other hand, had as his focus the realization of one generic American; thus his form was autobiographical. In his firmly democratic insistence on himself as representative of the equality of man, he is the closest of all our major prose writers in spirit and in rhythm to Walt Whitman, who attempted to sing America by celebrating himself and in the process of so doing created a new self who was that of representational America. Wolfe's form is that of the *Bildungsroman,* or apprenticeship, novel. The central search which his characters are embarked upon is a search for what he once called "surety" and that he symbolically represented as "the search for the Father"—[84] that is, a search for a home in a homeless land, a search for communion in a lonely world, the endless and always unfruitful quest for the lost leaf, the stone, the unfound door which leads out of the self into the surrounding brotherhood of man.

Wolfe's memory was, as he declared, unusually sensitive to the sounds, the colors, the odors, the palpable realities of the world around him; and his own deeply felt emotions, his sense both of embarrassment and of surprise at the nature of his heritage, combined with this lyric quality to bring the real world vigorously to bear upon the nerve ends of his readers, made his first novel *Look Homeward, Angel* a book in structure not unlike Joyce's *Portrait of the Artist as a Young Man,* although it differs in the intensity with which he defines and describes himself.

Wolfe and Faulkner share this intensity, as they also share the verbal pyrotechnics of which each is capable. Both writers can wrap language into special forms and out of these special forms create new, fresh, and original meanings. Wolfe is pre-eminently a stylist, a lyric and rhetorical poet. He was influenced in terms of structure and language by James Joyce, Dostoevski, George Bernard Shaw, Sinclair Lewis, H. G. Wells, and Marcel Proust. Yet his large works were diffuse and uncertain. His sentences are complex and intricately interwoven, and his adjectives and adverbs are rich, various, and extravagant. Yet Wolfe is a writer of remarkably direct sensory sensation and great clarity of utterance. There is a fundamental difference in the way in which Wolfe uses language from that in which Faulkner uses it. In Faulkner's case the syntax of the sentence often proves an inadequate container for the intensity of the words, and his great sprawling sentences run on and on and on. The tone of Faulkner's voice becomes loud, even, on many occasions, strident, and his complexity is one of symbol, of *leit-motif,* of image, and above all of cadence and rhythm. We encounter its difficulties immediately and must wrestle with them with some success before we get to the inner core of his work. Though Wolfe has many of these qualities, he also has them under a kind of control quite different from that of Faulkner, for Wolfe's sentences are seldom—very seldom indeed—difficult; and when they present us with special words or special constructions, it is usually in those few passages where the influence of James Joyce and *Ulysses* is most plainly before us. Wolfe can write with so great a crystal clarity and directness that it becomes simply the transmission of a palpable world. Both those who praise and those who condemn Wolfe see in him two kinds of writer—the writer of the lyric poem in which the physical world has a palpability as great as it has in the work of any American writer and the writer of dythrambic prose passages of great power and subtlety and frequently of great effectiveness, but which on more than one occasion degenerate into bombast.

Wolfe's difficulties are not on the surface but are in the interrelationships, frequently difficult to see, which he is attempting to establish through the record of a individual experience. George Webber said in *You Can't Go Home Again*, "I'm looking for a way . . . I think it may be something like what people vaguely mean when they speak of fiction. A kind of legend, perhaps. Something—a story—composed of all the knowledge I have, of all the living I've seen. Not the facts, you understand—not just the record of my life—but something truer than the facts —something distilled out of my experience and transmitted into a form of universal application."[85]

Wolfe's remarkable success with the control of narrative is best realized in the briefer forms of the short story and the short novel. Those who claim that Wolfe could not conduct a narrative with skill and grace simply have not looked with care at such works as *A Portrait of Bascom Hawke* or "*I Have a Thing To Tell You*" or *The Web of Earth*. However, these individual experiences ultimately are important not in themselves but in terms of the impact which they make upon their communicating narrator; and in all of Wolfe's work the final meaning of this communicating narrator, whatever name we call him by, is nebulous and hazy. Wolfe very often has taken magnificent dramatic and satiric portions of his work, has fragmented them, and has distributed them over the pages of Gant's and Webber's experiences and lost for them some of their intrinsic unity and much of their force.

There is only one real subject of Wolfe's work, and that subject is the American self, whether it is called Eugene Gant or George Webber; and this personality is the product in very direct ways of the experiences which Wolfe has had. Many of these illuminating and instructive experiences are ones in which George Webber or Eugene Gant does not directly participate except as spectator and commentator.

This pattern of development for Eugene Gant and George Webber is grounded in the South, but it is grounded in a South which is steadily expanding outward, if that South is known through the protagonist of the novels. Wolfe himself was born in a hill-encircled mountain town at a time when it was moving from the long somnolence of the late nineteenth century into the frenzied activity of the commercialized twentieth century. From this hill-bound home he came some 250 miles to Chapel Hill and entered the University of North Carolina at a time when that institution was shaking off its languor as a liberal arts college and was beginning to create for itself and for its students a new image and a new meaning based upon serious critical research into the nature of its region. Wolfe was a part of, and himself contributed significantly to, the movement which lifted the University of North Carolina at Chapel Hill from a provincial college to a national university. He left Chapel Hill to go to Harvard and become there a student of John Livingston Lowes and of George Pierce Baker, whose 47 Drama Workshop Wolfe worked in. From Cambridge he moved to New York City where he taught in New York University. From there he moved on more than one occasion to Europe; and as he moved backwards and forwards between the South, New York, and Europe, his life assumed a steadily expanding pattern, and his interest in his nation became increasingly greater. That he died of a disease contracted on the North Pacific Coast of the United States is to some extent an indication of the way in which the self, which for him was a receiving and defining order, is still in control of the writer and is shaping the direction and the destiny of his work, although, even at the end, it is still unable to give it firm and controlling form.

His structures, like those of Whitman, were loose enough to include almost everything but not firm enough to give effective control to what they included. The result is that Wolfe wrote some the finest individual scenes produced by an American in this century but did not produce a single book after his first one which in itself merits such lofty claims.

I do not believe that this failure is the result of Wolfe's alienation from his culture or his separation from the South, but I do believe that had he lived he would perhaps have found an organizing principle within which his works could find unity and that principle would have been national, not regional. Yet, as Faulkner observed,[86] it is futile to weep about the absence of books which were never written because the author, in Poe's phrase, is "doubly dead in that he died so young."

The attitude which Wolfe took toward his own region was certainly not a very friendly one despite the real affection that in many ways he had for it. In leaving the South he felt that he was taking leave of a group of people who were part of his blood and birth but of whom he could

say, ". . . the Joyners were a race as lawless as the earth,
as criminal as nature. They hurled their prodigal seed
into the raw earth of a mountain woman's body, bringing
to life a swarming progeny which lived or died, was ex-
tinguished in its infancy or fought its way triumphantly to
maturity against the savage enemies of poverty, ignorance,
and squalor which menaced it at every step. They bloomed
or perished as things live or die in nature—but the triumphant Joyners, superior to all loss or waste, lived forever
as a river lives. Other tribes of men came up out of the
earth, flourished for a space, and then, engulfed and
falling, went back into the earth from which they came.
Only the Joyners—these horror-hungry, time-devouring
Joyners—lived, and would not die."[87] He summarized
George Webber's life and the pull between South and
North by the web of earth and the rock of the city in these
words, "Thus, day by day, in the taut and tangled web of
this boy's life, the two hemispheres that touched but never
joined, contended separated, recombined, and wove again.
First came the old dark memory of time-haunted man and
the lost voices in the hills a hundred years ago, the world-
lost and hill-haunted sorrow of the time-triumphant
Joyners. Then his spirit flamed beyond the hills, beyond
lost time and sorrow, to his father and his father's earth;
and when he thought of him his heart grew warm, the
hot blood thudded in his veins, he lept all barriers of the
here and now, and northward, gleaming brightly there
beyond the hills, he saw a vision of the golden future in
new lands."[88]

In *The Web and the Rock* this outward extension of
the self is most nearly comprehended in the action of a
single novel. The story of Monk Webber begins with his
childhood of dreaming perceptions of beauty, a beauty
which was suddenly interrupted by the inherent violence
which underlay his world and which is symbolized by the

explosive, mad, and murderous eruption of the Negro Dick Prosser in the chapter "Child by Tiger." He moves on to Pine Rock College, where his most significant actions were his choosing Dostoevski over Dickens and attending a football victory over Virginia. Then he goes to New York City, and there, as he tries to write, he comes to believe "that every man on earth held in the little tenement of his flesh and spirit the whole ocean of human life and time, and that he must drown in this ocean unless, somhow, he 'got it out of him'—unless he mapped and charted it, fenced and defined it, plumbed it to its uttermost depths, and knew it to its smallest pockets upon the remotest shores of the everlasting earth."[89] He goes to Europe and meets and falls in love with the Jewess Mrs. Esther Jack and continues the affair back in America. He goes back to Europe, engages in a fight in Munich at the Oktoberfest, and, while recovering in a hospital, comes to his moment of self-knowledge—the knowledge that limitations must be accepted, that "we who are men are more than men, and less than spirit." He knows that the "web" of the Southland home has been broken. His thoughts turn back to the recollection of the childhood dream—"and morning, morning in the thickets of the memory, and so many lives-and-deaths of life so long ago, together with the thought of Winter howling in the oak, so many sunlights that had come and gone since morning, morning, and all lost voices—'Son, where are you?'—of lost kinsmen in the mountains long ago. . . . That was a good time then."[90] But he knows, too, that "you can't go home again."

Now his liberated, Whitmanesque imagination can stretch over the whole continent and seek out, as he does in *You Can't Go Home Again*, the representative American. This American is struggling upward in his world and reaching out to realize himself—he is vicariously a Negro boy in South Chicago, remembering the "lost and buried South" and dreaming of success as a prizefighter. He is vicariously a boy in "the clay-baked piedmont of the South" dreaming of greatness as a baseball player. He is vicariously a Jewish boy in "the East-Side Ghetto of Manhattan" in an "agony of concentration" struggling to become a great scientist. Thus the giant web is broken and Wolfe now can reach out and declare, "So, then, to every man his chance—to every man, regardless of his birth, his shining, golden opportunity—to every man the right to live, to work, to be himself, and to become whatever thing his manhood and his vision can combine to make him—this, seeker, is the promise of America."[91]

Faulkner and Wolfe shared many things—being "Southern," verbal power, intensity, probing introspection—but they differed in significant ways. For Faulkner was the novelist of the rural South and its traditions of social order, and Wolfe was the spokesman of the New South, the South which was embracing the future of industrialism and capitalism and whose sons dream of great cities and the vast nation. Thus, where Faulkner used a rural county and the material around it to write a cosmic tragedy, Wolfe sought in his pages to show through the experience of one man what it meant to be American. Faulkner's characters are embedded in history; Wolfe's are dramatizations of attitudes that are national and epic rather than sectional and mythic. Wolfe's fiction was determined by the Piedmont middle-class world which he knew. When he moved from it, he moved outward to embrace the nation and to attempt to realize the promise of America. That his work has both the evocative power and the fragmentary nature of Whitman's *Leaves of Grass* is an indication of how thoroughly he had moved outside his hill-pent home to a position from which he could declare:

"I think the true fulfillment of our spirit, of our people, of our mighty and immortal land, is yet to come. I think the true discovery of our democracy is still before us. And I think that all these things are certain as the morning, as inevitable as noon."[92]

Three Views of the Real

> . . . if [a novelist] believes that actions are prede-
> termined by psychic make-up or the economic situa-
> tion or some other determinable factor, then he will
> be concerned above all with an accurate reproduction
> of the things that most immediately concern man,
> with the natural forces that he feels control his
> destiny. Such a writer may produce a great tragic
> naturalism, for by his responsibility to the things he
> sees, he may transcend the limitations of his narrow
> vision.   *Flannery O'Connor*[93]

THE MEANING OF A WORK OF ART IS INEXTRICABLY INTER-
woven from language, character, action, and form; and
our ultimate comprehension of the fundamental value of
a work of fiction rests upon our seeing it as an organic
whole. In every work of art four elements are present:
the subject, which in Aristotle's sense we can view as the
thing being imitated; the artist who is using his work as
an expression of his personal vision of man; the audience,
which through the work of art catches some glimpse of
the artist's vision of experience; and finally, the work
itself independent of all of these things, an artifact with

an objective reality. In these essays I have placed a primary emphasis upon the mimetic quality in Southern writing because it seems to me that many critics of contemporary Southern fiction have failed to recognize the significant variations in its subject.

I have also made a serious effort to look at the author himself, for, as Wayne Booth has forcefully reminded us,[94] the author is always present in a work of fiction; and even when he thinks he has withdrawn himself, like James Joyce's artist, who "like the God of the creation, remains within or behind or beyond or above his handiwork, invisible, refined out of existence, indifferent, paring his fingernails,"[95] the very fact of his indifference is a part of his reality; and try as he will fingernail clippings will get mixed in the work. The authors of Southern fiction have made relatively little effort to "deal themselves out of the game" as far as the reader is concerned, and they are always present and willing to use any of many kinds of devices to control and to shape the response of the reader. They are there through attitude toward subjects; they are there through direct authorial statement; and they are pervasively there through style.

All authors manipulate language to their own purposes —Miss Glasgow did so wittily; William Faulkner, with incantatory power; and Thomas Wolfe, lyrically and directly through image and adjective. Miss Glasgow's theme is domestic, and she operates within the relatively closed circle of a small group of families, using as her focus elderly, gracious, ceremonious but ineffectual men and as her central situation the position of marriage and of women and their place in society. William Faulkner deals with a broad spectrum of the social world, however small the rural Mississippi stage is upon which it is enacted, covering, according to his famous map, 2,400 square miles and a population of 6,298 whites and 9,313 Negroes. To

that legend, he also added, "William Faulkner, sole owner
and proprietor"; but throughout the more than twenty
volumes of his fiction, he has convinced a substantial portion of the reading world that most of the fundamental
situations which man faces are somehow duplicated on
Faulkner's "postage stamp of earth" and are, therefore,
as much theirs as Faulkner's. Thomas Wolfe, on the other
hand, was trying to grasp within himself the largest possible range of experience, both real and vicarious; and he
defined generic man not as a Southerner but as an American so that at last he could say as Walt Whitman did,

> I sing myself, and celebrate myself,
> And what I assume you shall assume,
> For every atom belonging to me as good belongs to you.[96]

Miss Glasgow centered her work in large measure upon
the definition of this mannered Southern society because
she was a resident of the seaboard and an ironic critic of
its way of life. Out of its conventions, she made the novel
of manners and tested the virtues and the vices of her
characters by those "memorials of old traditions." Faulkner, tracing the long history of Yoknapatawpha County,
moved back into the past and attempted the evocation of
legend and the creation of intense symbolic statements.
For his characters the past lives with passion and enormous
demands. Many of his characters are like the Reverend
Gail Hightower in *Light in August,* who "grew to manhood among phantoms, and side by side with a ghost. The
phantoms were his father, his mother, and an old Negro
woman. . . . It was as though the very cold and uncompro-
mising conviction which propped it upright, as it were,
between puritan and cavalier, had become not defeated
and not discouraged, but wiser" and who hears the gallop-
ing horses of his soldier father's company, "the wild bugles
and the clashing sabres and the dying thunder of hooves";[97]
and out of this past Faulkner has created the materials of a

cosmic fable. Thomas Wolfe alone of these writers has felt the democratic pressures which de Tocqueville defined, and he has written more of himself than of his society.

The writers whom we are looking at here have handled the Southern past in three radically different ways. Speaking for the Tidewater, Ellen Glasgow has viewed Southern history as fact. She had tried to portray in the characters closest to its catastrophe the created illusion that it did not happen, as she did in *The Deliverance;* but she and her characters know that however much defeat might be screened away from the consciousness of a dying patrician lady, it could not be screened away from her children. She has used the fact of this past as a novelist of manners does, that is, as the means through which a social world is given ironic commentary. She prescribed for the South that she loved and was amused at her now classic formula of "blood and irony" and wrote of it as closer to New England than any other portion of the New World. In her Queenborough novels she portrays the way in which it continues to pay lip service to ideals that have lost their cause for existence and to surrender hope and energy to a social structure whose meaning and justification ended long ago. Thus, like John Marquand's patrician Bostonians or Santayana's *Last Puritan,* her people represent decayed and ineffectual patricians.

On the other hand, the past for William Faulkner has been a world of fable raised almost to the order of myth; and he has used it, as George Snell saw many years ago, as an apocalyptic vision. The Deep South has dealt with the dream of the Tidewater in extravagant terms since the 1830's, and in Faulkner's work this same intense extravagance appears. Passionate and overdrawn, his characters loom not like figures who rode with Stuart or marched with Pickett but like vast shadowy forms who would have been equally at home in the Greek theatre and who are closer to Sophocles and Euripides than they are to Stark Young or Margaret Mitchell.

For Thomas Wolfe the past was of much less importance. He declared of the Tidewater gentry, "their pretense is reduced to pretending that they amounted to so much formerly. And they really amounted to very little."[98] Wolfe's view of the present state of the Low Country and the Tidewater culture is one which Miss Glasgow has treated in her ironic comedies. The pretense regarding what that culture still is has seldom received more effective reduction than it has endured under Miss Glasgow's scalpel. Yet she would have denied, and I think Faulkner for his world, too, would have denied, that the pretense rested, as Wolfe insisted, on very little. Each—that is, Tidewater and Deep South—knew that an order had existed, a structure had been there in society, and, though it might today be gone, it could not ever be totally and completely forgotten. Only Wolfe of the three believed that past to be of relatively little value.

It is interesting to see how each of these novelists treats the central fact of Southern history—that is, the Civil War. There can be little question that each of them sees this War as the watershed in the social and economic history of the South, but each of them also takes a peculiarly different attitude toward it. Miss Glasgow's is ironic. The Civil War cut away the basic roots out of which the Tidewater manners had come; and after the War, these manners and conventions, no longer descriptive of an inner reality, became desiccated and seered. War was thus for her a great accelerator of change. One of her most effective pictures of its meaning is through the character Mrs. Blake in *The Deliverance*. Mrs. Blake, a very elderly and gracious lady, lived on after the War ignorant of its outcome and protected from such disastrous knowledge by her children at great cost to themselves in order that she,

unaware of how her world had changed, could, as Miss
Glasgow says that she and all Virginia did, "cling, with
passionate fidelity, to the ceremonial forms of tradition."[99]

For Thomas Wolfe the Civil War is simply a fact and
not a particularly significant one, one perhaps to be forgotten. It does not grieve upon the bones of his own world;
and when he turns, as on occasion he does, to a descrip-
tion of those who would insist upon the beauty and the
value of the pre-Civil War South, he turns to an ironic
treatment of cherished dignity. The picture which he
paints of the "refined young gentlemen of the New Confederacy" is one that only a person unsympathetic to
both the past and the present South could have uttered.[100]
In *You Can't Go Home Again,* Wolfe has George Webber
say, "Sometimes it seems to me . . . that America went
off the track somewhere—back around the time of Civil
War, or pretty soon afterwards. Instead of going ahead
and developing along the line in which the country started
out, it got shunted off in another direction—and now we
look around and see we've gone places we didn't mean to
go. Suddenly we realize that America has turned into
something ugly—and vicious—and corroded at the heart of
its power with easy wealth and graft and special privilege."[101]

In contrast, William Faulkner in *Intruder in the Dust*
says: "For every Southern boy fourteen years old, not once
but whenever he wants it, there is the instant when it's
still not two o'clock on that July afternoon in 1863, the
brigades are in position behind the rail fence, the guns
are laid and ready in the woods and the furled flags are
already loosened to break out and Pickett himself with his
long oiled ringlets and his hat in one hand probably and
his sword in the other looking up the hill waiting for
Longstreet to give the word and it's all in the balance, it
hasn't happened yet, it hasn't even begun."[102]

Another way to see a difference clearly demonstrated

among the writers using these three Souths as their subject is to compare James Branch Cabell's mocking and
ironic autobiography *Let Me Lie,* in which the customs
and attitudes of the Tidewater are held up to gently
mocking laughter, with William Alexander Percy's autobiography *Lanterns on the Levee,* in which his romantic
sense of the beauty and dignity of Southern traditional
life—even while some of its values and standards are
questioned—casts over it some of the glow that Stark Young
embodied in *So Red the Rose.* Against this view of the
South, we might juxtapose the image which Thomas Wolfe
used in *The Web and the Rock* to sum up "the whole dark
picture of those decades of defeat and darkness." George
Webber sees an old house overgrown with grass and weeds
so that its paths are no longer passable and no one visits
it again, and an old man walks into the house never to
come out again. The house shines faintly "like its own
ruined spectre, its doors and windows black as eyeless
sockets. That was the South. That was the South for thirty
years or more." But significantly for Thomas Wolfe his
generation has come "into a kind of sunlight of another
century. They had come out upon the road again. The
road was being paved. More people came now. They cut
a pathway to the door again. Some of the weeds were
clear. Another house was built . . . and the world was
in."[108] This house is not unlike Sutpen's mansion in
Absalom, Absalom! But Faulkner's house is enveloped in
flames before the imprisoned past (in the person of Henry
Sutpen) can come out into the modern world.

This view of a new South was alien to Miss Glasgow,
who could declare, "Noise, numbers, size, quantity, all are
exerting their lively or sinister influence. Sentiment no
longer suffices. To be Southern, even to be solid, is not
enough; for the ambition of the new South is not to be
self-sufficing, but to be more Western than the West and

more American than the whole of America. Uniformity, once despised and rejected, has become the established ideal. Satisfied for so long to leave the miscellaneous product 'Americanism' to the rest of the country, the South is at last reaching out for its neglected inheritance."[104] She could have been thinking of Thomas Wolfe.

The first of our twentieth century major Southern novelists, Ellen Glasgow, took as her subject the fixed social world of the Tidewater and took as her theme the restrictions placed upon character through the pressure of a decaying, traditionalized, formal society. At one time the society she describes had had grace, dignity, beauty, and honor, but that day had been lost in the early eras of its history. After the Civil War, confronted with the rising lower middle class, it had created itself into a sentimentalized evasion of the world and had made manners a means of excluding reality from the central assumptions by which its citizens lived. Like Jenny Blair Archbald, Miss Glasgow's characters could ignore the true implications of the world in which they lived by falling back upon a set of conventionalized evasions; but like Jenny, too, this world could step aside from the consequences of its acts only at a tragic cost to its fellow men. Ellen Glasgow knew, as Edith Wharton had known,[105] that a trivial society can be effectively described only in terms of what it destroys. Whatever shadow of evil hangs over her world, it hangs alike over old General Archbald and young Jenny Blair, for each has accepted a system in which the death of the personality is the price of acceptance in the society. In presenting this world, Miss Glasgow has used the well-made realistic novel of manners; and when her voice is heard, as it is on almost every page she wrote, it is a very urbane, witty, and ironic voice, for like Thackeray before her she not only condemns her *Vanity Fair* but is part of what she condemns.

William Faulkner in the lush, semi-tropical Deep South found material appropriate to gothic treatment and used it to create a symbolic picture of the South as an historical myth and as a cosmic tragedy. His plots are melodramatic structures that are very close to the detective story, as Greek tragedy was, for like the detective story and Greek tragedy the plots move forward to those crucial recognition scenes in which the character comes finally to perceive a truth previously hidden from him.

Thomas Wolfe speaks directly of the Piedmont South, a modern world in which the triumph of the middle class has forced a pattern of values primarily in terms of size, cost, and chromium; but he is, despite his criticism of its lack of standards and of beauty, an advocate of the new South, a region willing both to accept and to profit from the general character of his nation; and early in his novels and in his career Wolfe abandoned "hill-pent" Asheville to seek not a regional but a national meaning and to find in himself the common experiences of all men. Hence, his books become the loosely constructed auto-biographical record of an intense and lyric search for reality as it expresses itself in the inner character of the American. The bardic quality is very clearly in his work for he approaches himself and his subject primarily as an epic poet and only very partially as a novelist.

These three writers have established, thus, three modes tied in intimate ways to the regions which produced them and viewing in different lights the past history out of which they came. These modes might be defined in any of several different ways. Ellen Glasgow's could well be called the urbane; William Faulkner's the daemonic; and Thomas Wolfe's, the intense. Viewed in another way, we would see Miss Glasgow as a realist and her approach toward Southern society as ironic. We would see Faulkner as a romanticist and his approach to Southern history and

society as symbolic and mythic; and we would see Wolfe
as an epic lyricist and his view of the Southern society outside his self as satiric. Although Miss Glasgow is correct in
asserting that "the truth of art and the truth of life are two
different truths,"[106] certainly their artistic uses by these
writers define the basic and perhaps ineradicable differences in what we loosely call "The South."

Four years before her death, the gallant lady and mili-
tant Christian, Flannery O'Connor, spoke movingly on the
difficulty and challenge of being a Southern writer and
brought the essentially private vision of the novelist into
effective relation with the nature of his subject. She said:
"The problem for [a Southern] novelist will be to know
how far he can distort without destroying, and in order
not to destroy, he will have to descend far enough into
himself to reach those underground springs that give life
to his work. This descent into himself will, at the same
time, be a descent into his region. It will be a descent
through the darkness of the familiar into a world where
like the blind man cured in the gospels, he sees men as if
they were trees, but walking. This is the beginning of
vision, and I feel it is a vision which we in the South must
at least try to understand if we want to participate in the
continuance of a vital Southern literature. I hate to think
that in twenty years Southern writers too may be writing
about men in grey flannel suits and may have lost their
ability to see that these gentlemen are even greater freaks
that [sic] what we are writing about now. I hate to think of
the day when the Southern writer will satisfy the tired
reader."[107]

I feel that neither "the man in the grey flannel suit"
nor "the tired reader" is likely to stop the efforts of good
writers from all three Souths to find in region, race, religion, and physical reality a viable subject for the statement
of unpalatable but enduring truths.

Notes

1. H. A. Taine, *History of English Literature*, translated into English by H. Van Laun (4 vols, Philadelphia, 1908). First published as *Histoire de la litterature anglaise* (Paris, 1864).

2. Edmund Wilson, *The Bit Between My Teeth* (New York, 1965), p. 2.

3. Taine, *History of English Literature*, pp. 17-25.

4. Ellen Glasgow, *A Certain Measure* (New York, 1943), p. 167.

5. Alfred H. Korzybski, *Science and Sanity: An Introduction to Non-Aristotelian Systems and General Semantics* (Lancaster, Pa., 1933).

6. C. Vann Woodward, "The Irony of Southern History," *The Burden of Southern History* (Baton Rouge, 1960), pp. 167-191.

7. W. J. Cash, *The Mind of the South* (New York, 1954), pp. 22, 23.

8. C. Hugh Holman, "Ellen Glasgow and the Southern Literary Tradition," *Virginia in History and Tradition*, edited by R. C. Simonini, Jr. (Farmville, Virginia, 1958), reprinted in *Southern Writers: Appraisals in Our Time*, edited by R. C. Simonini, Jr. (Charlottesville, Virginia, 1964), pp. 103-123; C. Hugh Holman, "The Dark, Ruined Helen of His Blood: Thomas Wolfe and the South," *South: Modern Southern Literature in its Cultural Setting*, edited by Louis D. Rubin, Jr., and Robert D. Jacobs (Garden City, N. Y., 1961), pp. 177-197; C. Hugh Holman, "A Cycle of Change in Southern Literature," *The South in Continuity and Change*, edited by John C. McKinney and Edgar T. Thompson (Durham, N. C., 1965), pp. 384-403.

9. Flannery O'Connor, "The Fiction Writer and His Country," *The Living Novel: A Symposium*, edited by Granville Hicks (New York, 1962), p. 160.

10. Robert Penn Warren, "William Faulkner," *Forms of Modern Fiction*, edited by William Van O'Connor (Minneapolis, Minn., 1948), pp. 125-143; Cleanth Brooks, *William Faulkner: The Yoknapatawpha Country* (New Haven, 1963).

11. Thomas Wolfe, *The Web and the Rock* (New York, 1939), p. 242.

84   *Three Modes of Modern Southern Fiction*

12. Ellen Glasgow, *The Sheltered Life* (Garden City, N. Y. 1932), p. 98.
13. Henry Adams, *The United States in 1800* (Ithaca, N. Y., 1955), p. 107. (A reprint of Chapters I-VI of Adams' *History of the United States During the Administrations of Jefferson and Madison*, 9 vols., Boston, 1889-1891).
14. Thomas J. Wertenbaker, *The Golden Age of Colonial Culture* (Ithaca, N. Y., 1959), p. 3.
15. John Pendleton Kennedy, *Swallow Barn; or, A Sojourn in the Old Dominion* (New York, 1962), p. 27.
16. Thomas Nelson Page, *The Old South: Essays Social and Political* (New York, 1927), p. 5.
17. Glasgow, *A Certain Measure*, p. 155.
18. Edward Wagenknecht, *The Cavalcade of the American Novel* (New York, 1952), p. 348.
19. Glasgow, *A Certain Measure*, p. 135.
20. *Ibid.*, p. 142.
21. *Ibid.*, p. 4.
22. Daniel W. Patterson, "Ellen Glasgow's Plan for a Social History of Virginia," *Modern Fiction Studies*, V (Winter, 1960), 353-360; and the reply by Oliver L. Steele, "Ellen Glasgow, Social History, and the 'Virginia Edition'," *Modern Fiction Studies*, VI (Summer, 1961), 173-176.
23. Glasgow, *The Sheltered Life*, p. 26.
24. Glasgow, *A Certain Measure*, p. 5.
25. H. Blair Rouse, ed. *Letters of Ellen Glasgow* (New York, 1958), p. 342.
26. Glasgow, *A Certain Measure*, p. 75.
27. *Ibid.*, p. 28.
28. *Ibid.*, pp. 237, 238.
29. Glasgow, *The Sheltered Life*, p. 193.
30. Ellen Glasgow, *The Romantic Comedians* (Garden City, N. Y., 1926), p. 2.
31. *Ibid.*, pp. 3-4.
32. *Ibid.*, p. 3.
33. *Ibid.*, pp. 20, 218.
34. *Ibid.*, p. 251.
35. Glasgow, *A Certain Measure*, pp. 209-210.
36. Rouse, *Letters of Ellen Glasgow*, p. 232.
37. *Ibid.*, p. 124.
38. Glasgow, *The Sheltered Life*, p. 152.
39. *Ibid.*, pp. 163-164.
40. *Ibid.*, p. 283.
41. Rouse, *Letters of Ellen Glasgow*, pp. 124, 262.
42. Glasgow, *A Certain Measure*, pp. 224-225.
43. Glasgow, *The Sheltered Life*, p. 155.
44. Glasgow, *A Certain Measure*, p. 147.
45. William Faulkner, "The Bear" in *Go Down, Moses* (New York, 1942), p. 293.
46. Cash, *The Mind of the South*, p. 42.
47. C. Hugh Holman, "Introduction," *Views and Review of American Literature, History, and Fiction* by William Gilmore Simms (Cambridge, Mass., 1962); and C. Hugh Holman, "Introduction," *The Yemassee* by William Gilmore Simms (Boston, 1961). See also the "Notes of a Small Tourist" letters to the *City Gazette*, in *The Letters of William Gilmore Simms*, edited by Mary C. S. Oliphant, A. T. Odell, and T. C. D. Eaves (Columbia, S. C., 1952), I, 10-38.
48. Malcolm Cowley, "Introduction," *The Portable Faulkner* (New York, 1946).
49. Richard P. Adams, "The Apprenticeship of William Faulkner," *Tulane Studies in English*, XII (1962), 113-156.
50. Randall Stewart, "Hawthorne and Faulkner," *College English*, XVII (February, 1956); William

Notes

Van O'Connor, "Hawthorne and Faulkner: Some Common Ground," *Virginia Quarterly Review*, XXXIII (Winter, 1957).

51. Adams, "The Apprenticeship of William Faulkner," pp. 142-146.

52. George Snell, "Apocalyptics," *The Shapers of American Fiction* (New York, 1947), pp. 32-104; particularly pp. 87-104.

53. Irving Howe, *William Faulkner: A Critical Study*, Revised edition, (New York, 1960), pp. 8-9.

54. Cleanth Brooks, *William Faulkner: The Yoknapatawpha Country*, p. 295.

55. William Faulkner, *Absalom, Absalom!* (New York, 1936), p. 385. (This map was re-drawn and used in *The Viking Portable Faulkner* and the Modern Library edition of *Absalom, Absalom!)*

56. *Ibid.*, p. 379.

57. *Ibid.*, p. 221.

58. *Ibid.*, pp. 228-229.

59. *Ibid.*, pp. 377-378.

60. Frederick L. Gwynn and Joseph L. Blotner, editors, *Faulkner in the University* (New York, 1965), p. 71.

61. *Ibid.*, p. 73.

62. *Ibid.*, p. 75.

63. *Ibid*, p. 80.

64. *Ibid.*, pp. 273-274.

65. *Ibid.*, p. 35.

66. Faulkner, *Absalom, Absalom!*, p. 141.

67. Gwynn and Blotner, *Faulkner in the University*, p. 94.

68. Ernest Hemingway, *Death in the Afternoon* (New York, 1932), p. 2.

69. Wolfe, *The Web and the Rock*, p. 262.

70. *Thomas Wolfe's Letters to His Mother*, edited by John S. Terry (New York, 1943), p. 50.

71. Wolfe, *The Web and the Rock*, p. 13.

72. *Ibid.*, pp. 13-14.

73. *Ibid.*, p. 15.

74. *Ibid.*, pp. 16-17.

75. Thomas Wolfe, *Look Homeward, Angel* (New York, 1929), p. 626.

76. Alexis de Tocqueville, *Democracy in America*, translated by Henry Reeves, corrected and edited with historical essay, notes, and bibliographies by Phillips Bradley (New York, 1957), Part II, pp. 80-81.

77. James Fenimore Cooper, *Notions of the American* (Philadelphia, 1828), Letter XXIII.

78. Rob Roy Purdy, ed. *Fugitive's Reunion: Conversations at Vanderbilt, May 3-5, 1956* (Nashville, Tenn., 1959), p. 34.

79. Ralph Waldo Emerson, "The Poet," in *Essays, Second Series* (Boston, 1844).

80. Wolfe, *Look Homeward Angel*, p. 3.

81. *Ibid.*, p. 2.

82. Wolfe, *The Web and the Rock*, p. 246.

83. Thomas Wolfe, *Of Time and the River* (New York, 1935), pp. 866-869.

84. Thomas Wolfe, *The Story of a Novel* (New York, 1936), p. 39.

85. Thomas Wolfe, *You Can't Go Home Again* (New York, 1941), pp. 386-387.

86. In a letter quoted by Richard Walser in the Introduction to his collection, *The Enigma of Thomas Wolfe: Biographical and Critical Selections* (Cambridge, Mass., 1953), p. vii.

87. Wolfe, *The Web and the Rock*, p. 83.

88. *Ibid.*, p. 90.

89. *Ibid.*, p. 262.

90. *Ibid.*, p. 695.

91. Wolfe, *You Can't Go Home Again*, p. 508.

92. *Ibid.*, p. 741.

93. Flannery O'Connor, "Some Aspects of the Grotesque in Southern Literature," *Cluster Review* (Mercer University), Seventh Issue (March, 1965), p. 6.

94. Wayne C. Booth, *Rhetoric of Fiction* (Chicago, 1961). The division of a work of art into four elements is drawn from Meyer Abrams. *The Mirror and the Lamp* (New York, 1953).

95. James Joyce, *Portrait of an Artist as a Young Man,* in *The Portable James Joyce,* edited by Harry Levin (New York, 1947), pp. 481-482.

96. Walt Whitman, "Song of Myself," lines 1-3.

97. William Faulkner, *Light in August* (New York, 1932), pp. 415, 422.

98. Wolfe, *The Web and the Rock,* p. 15.

99. Glasgow, *A Certain Measure,* p. 27.

100. Wolfe, *The Web and the Rock,* p. 242.

101. Wolfe, *You Can't Go Home Again,* p. 393.

102. William Faulkner, *Intruder in the Dust* (New York, 1948), pp. 194-195.

103. Wolfe, *The Web and the Rock,* pp. 245-246.

104. Glasgow, *A Certain Measure,* p. 145.

105. Edith Wharton, *A Backward Glance* (New York, 1934), p. 207.

106. Glasgow, *A Certain Measure,* p. 213.

107. O'Connor, "Some Aspects of the Grotesque in Southern Literature," p. 22.

Notes on Sources

THE FOOTNOTES MAKE SPECIFIC IDENTIFICATIONS OF DIRECT references and quotations in the text. The essays included in this volume, however, rest upon an interpretation of the character of the Southern geography and climate and the assumption that this geography and climate and the patterns of immigration, colonization, and westward movement in the South have developed distinctive patterns which are the result of these historical facts and physical circumstances. In arriving at this conclusion, I have drawn widely and freely upon the work of a number of people who have studied the nature of the South and of its history. My central thesis is an oversimplified statement of an extremely complex matter, and the particular position I take is one the guilt for which I would assign to no single person. It represents the accumulation of many ideas and attitudes, and perhaps none of those from whom I have learned the data on which my thesis rests would accept it in toto. Accordingly, I should like here to suggest in some very broad groupings the general sources which I have used in arriving at my position.

I am indebted for my treatment of the geographical and racial structure of the South to several sources. The two major ones are: Rupert B. Vance, *Human Geography of the South* (Chapel Hill, N. C., 1932), Part I, "Backgrounds: Physical and Cultural," pages 20-76; and Howard W. Odum, *Southern*

Regions of the United States (Chapel Hill, N. C., 1936), pages 1-244, with particular emphasis on pages 207-244. Also of value has been Rupert B. Vance, *All These People: The Nation's Human Resources in the South* (Chapel Hill, N. C., 1945); Almon E. Parkins, *The South: Its Economic-Geographic Development* (New York, 1938), particularly Parts I and II, "The Southern Environment" and "The Peopling of the South," pages 23-120; and Henry Savage, *Seeds of Time: The Background of Southern Thinking* (New York, 1959), particularly the first three chapters.

My interpretation of the cultures which have grown from these geographical differences and the patterns by which these cultures have been established rests upon several bases. I shall list the major sources of the ideas which I have been attempting to deal with, again insisting that none of these authors is to be held responsible for my use of their data. They are: William A. Schaper, *Sectionalism and Representation in South Carolina* in *Annual Report of the American Historical Association, 1900* (Washington, 1901), I, 237-463; John W. Dinsmore, *The Scotch-Irish in America* (Chicago, 1906); Thomas J. Wertenbaker, *Patrician and Plebian in Virginia: or, The Origin and Development of the Social Classes of the Old Dominion* (Charlottesville, Virginia, 1910); Archibald Henderson, *The Conquest of the Old South West (Virginia, Carolinas, Tennessee, and Kentucky), 1740-1790* (New York, 1920); William E. Dodd, *The Cotton Kingdom* (New Haven, 1921); Ulrich B. Phillips, *Life and Labor in the Old South* (Boston, 1929); Clement Eaton's important study, *Freedom of Thought in the Old South* (Durham, N. C., 1940), and his *A History of the Old South* (New York, 1949), *The Growth of Southern Civilization, 1790-1860* (New York, 1961), and *The Mind of the Old South* (Baton Rouge, 1963); Thomas Perkins Abernethy, *Three Virginia Frontiers* (Baton Rouge, 1940); the monumental *History of the South,* under the general editorship of Wendell H. Stephenson and E. Merton Coulter (ten volumes of which eight are published), and particularly Charles Sydnor's *Development of Southern Sectionalism, 1819-1848* (Baton Rouge, 1948) and Avery O. Craven's *Growth of Southern Nationalism, 1848-1861* (Baton Rouge, 1953); Frank Lawrence Owsley, *Plain Folk of the Old South* (Baton Rouge, 1949); Carl Bridenbaugh, *Myths and Realities:*

Societies of the Colonial South (Baton Rouge, 1952); Francis B. Simkins, *A History of the South* (New York, 1953); Charles Woodmason, *The Carolina Back Country on the Eve of the Revolution: The Journals and Other Writings of Charles Woodmason, Anglican Itinerant,* edited by Richard J. Hooker (Chapel Hill, N. C., 1953); William Francis Guess, *South Carolina: Annals of Pride and Protest* (New York, 1957); John Richard Alden, *The First South* (Baton Rouge, 1961), particularly Chapter I, "The First South," pages 3-32; and James G. Leyburn, *The Scotch-Irish: A Social History* (Chapel Hill, N. C., 1962), particularly Part III, "The Scotch-Irish in America," pages 157-325.

I have found of great value the various attempts at the understanding of the South made by C. Vann Woodward, including his volume in the *History of the South, The Origins of the New South, 1877-1913* (Baton Rouge, 1951), and particularly the collection of his interpretative essays, *The Burden of Southern History* (Baton Rouge, 1960). Without his example, I should probably never have inquired into the "received standard" view of the nature of the Southern subject matter which our writers have used, although I would disavow for him any responsibility for my conclusions. Also, in dealing with the intellectual history and growth of Southern attitudes as they find expression in Southern society, I have found extremely useful the provocative, but not-always-trustworthy, expressions of W. J. Cash in *The Mind of the South* (New York, 1941) and of Rollin G. Osterweis in *Romanticism and Nationalism in the Old South* (New Haven, 1949), where a vast amount of valuable information is assembled around an over-simplified view of the nature of the Southern experience. Valuable, too, has been William R. Taylor, *Cavalier and Yankee: The Old South and American National Character* (New York, 1961). I have also found stimulating Daniel J. Boorstin, *The Americans: The National Experience* (New York, 1965), particularly Part Four, "The Rooted and the Uprooted: Southerners, White and Black."

For the study of Southern literature, I have found indispensable the example and the work of Jay B. Hubbell, and particularly his *The South in American Literature* (Durham, N. C., 1948) and *Southern Life in Fiction* (Athens, Georgia, 1960). Of significant importance in my attempt to understand contemporary Southern fiction have been two collections edited by Louis D. Rubin, Jr., and Robert D. Jacobs, *Southern Renascence: The Literature of the Modern South* (Baltimore, 1953) and *South: Modern Southern Literature in Its Cultural Setting* (New York, 1960).

For Ellen Glasgow, the standard guide is William W. Kelley's *Ellen Glasgow: A Bibliography* (Charlottesville, Virginia, 1964), an excellent and invaluable volume. Miss Glasgow's work has been the subject of five book-length studies: Frederick P. W. McDowell, *Ellen Glasgow and the Ironic Art of Fiction* (Madison, Wisconsin, 1960), an accurate, adequate, but not too perceptive or critically discerning a treatment; H. Blair Rouse, *Ellen Glasgow* (New York, 1962), a brief, factual treatment which tends to over-estimate her work; Louis D. Rubin, Jr., *No Place on Earth: Ellen Glasgow and James Branch Cabell and Richmond-in-Virginia* (Austin, Texas, 1959), a short and not too friendly study; Louis Auchincloss, *Ellen Glasgow* (Minneapolis, 1963), an urbane and discerning study in the "University of Minnesota Pamphlets on American Writers' Series"; this essay is reprinted with only small changes in Mr. Auchincloss's collection, *Pioneers and Caretakers* (Minneapolis, 1965); and the recent and, in many respects, the best study, Joan Foster Santas, *Ellen Glasgow's American Dream* (Charlotesville, Virginia, 1965).

For William Faulkner, the best bibliographical guide is James B. Meriwether, *The Literary Career of William Faulkner: A Bibliographical Study* (Princeton, 1961). By all means, the finest, most inclusive, and factually exacting volume done on William Faulkner is Cleanth Brooks, *William Faulkner: The Yoknapatawpha Country* (New Haven, 1963), an indispensable volume—as is also the edition prepared by Frederick L. Gwynn and Joseph L. Blotner, *Faulkner in the University: Class Conferences at the University of Virginia, 1957-1958* (Charlottesville, Virginia, 1959), a record of some of Faulkner's comments on his own work. Also of importance are Walter J. Slatoff, *Quest for Failure: A Study of William Faulkner* (Ithaca, New York, 1960), a stimulating and skeptical examination of Faulkner's books, and Olga W. Vickery, *The Novels of William Faulkner: A Critical Interpretation* (Baton Rouge, 1959), a lucid examination of Faulkner's work. The collection made by Frederick J. Hoffman and Olga W.

Vickery, *William Faulkner: Three Decades of Criticism* (East Lansing, Michigan, 1960), is a useful assembly of some of the best Faulkner criticism to appear in magazines. As a brief guide to the Faulkner world, Dorothy Tuck's *Crowell's Hand-Book of Faulkner* (New York, 1964) is compact, accurate, and useful. Melvin Backman's "Sutpen and the South: A study of *Absalom, Absalom!*," *PMLA*, LXXX (December, 1965), 596-604, contains many valuable insights and, in its notes, an excellent bibliography. Since it appeared after this book was in complete final form, I was unable to utilize it in the preparation of these essays. The reader will find it very helpful in pursuing some of the matters dealt with here.

For Thomas Wolfe, the best bibliography, although it contains inaccuracies, is Elmer D. Johnson, *Of Time and Thomas Wolfe: A Bibliography With a Character Index of His Works* (New York, 1959). Wolfe is the subject of a major and penetrating inquiry into his literary career and the structure of his work by Richard S. Kennedy, *The Window of Memory: The Literary Career of Thomas Wolfe* (Chapel Hill, N. C., 1962). The biography by Elizabeth Nowell, *Thomas Wolfe: A Biography* (New York, 1960), is the most complete to date, although it is less than completely satisfactory and takes Wolfe's fiction as too literal an autobiographical statement. Andrew Turnbull is working on a biography which gives every promise of being the standard work when it is completed. Of special usefulness as a compact and no-nonsense assembly of data about Wolfe and his work is Bruce R. McElderry Jr.'s *Thomas Wolfe* (New York, 1964). Two collections of essays about Wolfe and his work have been assembled: one edited by Richard Walser, *The Enigma of Thomas Wolfe: Biographical and Critical Selections* (Cambridge, Massachusetts, 1953); the other by C. Hugh Holman, *The World of Thomas Wolfe* (New York, 1962). The extremely useful statement about his own career which Wolfe makes in *The Story of a Novel* (New York, 1936) can now be supplemented by *Thomas Wolfe's Purdue Speech*, edited by William Braswell and Leslie A. Field (Lafayette, Indiana, 1964). The relationship of Wolfe's work to the Southern environment can be examined in Floyd C. Watkins's *Thomas Wolfe's Characters: Portraits from Life* (Norman, Oklahoma, 1957). Two valuable critical studies are Louis D. Rubin, Jr., *Thomas Wolfe: The Weather of His*

Youth (Baton Rouge, 1955) and Herbert Muller, *Thomas Wolfe* (Norfolk, Conn., 1947). C. Hugh Holman has also assembled in *The Thomas Wolfe Reader* (New York, 1962) representative selections from Wolfe's finest efforts, and his *The Short Novels of Thomas Wolfe* (New York, 1961) displays a frequently neglected aspect of Wolfe's work.

Index

This index contains the names of persons and books used or referred to in the text proper, with the books listed under their authors' names. It does not list subjects, footnote references, or items from the "Notes on Sources."